W9-BZA-814

Pages 222-223

Pages 210-211

Pages 190-191

Pages 164-165

Pages 120-121

Pages 144-145

Pages 86-87

Pages 106-107

Pages 56-57

Page 237

Pages 20-21

300

REASONS TO LOVE
NEW YORK

Project Editor: Agnès Saint-Laurent
Art Direction & Design: Josée Amyotte
Graphic Design: Chantal Landry
Translation: Margaret Ruse, Louisa Sage,
   and Caitlin Stall-Paquet
Revision: Robert Ronald
Proofreading: Matthew Brown

EXCLUSIVE DISTRIBUTOR:

For Canada and the United States:
Simon & Schuster Canada
166 King Street East, Suite 300
Toronto, ON M5A 1J3
phone: (647) 427-8882
            1-800-387-0446
Fax: (647) 430-9446
simonandschuster.ca

**Catalogue data available from Bibliothèque
et Archives nationales du Québec**

WARNING

As a city thirsty for new trends, New York is constantly changing, which means that the lifespan of
bars, restaurants and hotels varies greatly. Right up
until this book went to print, I walked through the
city's neighborhoods time and time again to ensure
that the information was up to date. However, as
nothing is safe from the passing of time, know that
some establishments might have moved or shut
down when you'll be visiting New York. Menus,
prices, fees and business hours are provided as a
guideline and are also subject to change. Enjoy your
stay!

Follow Marie-Joëlle Parent on Instagram:
@mariejoelleparent

03-16

© 2016 Juniper Publishing,
division of the Sogides Group Inc.,
a subsidiary of Québecor Média Inc.
(Montreal, Quebec)

Legal deposit: 2015
National Library of Québec
National Library of Canada

ISBN 978-1-988002-32-3

 **Conseil des Arts   Canada Council
du Canada   for the Arts**

We gratefully acknowledge the support of the Canada
Council for the Arts for its publishing program.

We acknowledge the financial support of the
Government of Canada through the Canada Book Fund
for our publishing activities.

MARIE-JOËLLE PARENT

300

REASONS TO LOVE
NEW YORK

Contents

Introduction

My love for New York goes back to my very first trip to Manhattan at the end of the 1980s. I was barely eight years old, but I still remember the effect this thrilling city had on me. According to family legend, as we left the city, I turned around in the car's back seat and yelled: "Good-bye, New York! I'll be back!"

Fast-forward to 2009 when I came back for good. I had been named named New York correspondent by Quebecor Media, and I was going to begin my New York adventure. I'll always remember the January night when I set my suitcases down in an empty apartment of a high-rise in the very heart of Manhattan. Alone in the middle of a room lit by Times Square's neon lights, I understood that my life had just taken a crucial turn.

Being a journalist in the Big Apple is the greatest passport. The city's doors open and invitations pour out. As for the streets, they become a world to explore. Over six years, I discovered countless events and explored the city inside and out on foot, by bike and by subway.

After accumulating hundreds of addresses in my notebook, falling for place after place and meeting unforgettable people, I got the idea to share, in collection-form, my 300 reasons to love this astounding city. They're the things that made me fall in love with New York a little more each day. It's a book about restaurants, cafes, museums, hotels, boats, buildings, streets and people, all rolled into one.

Listed by neighborhood, these various reasons to "fall in love" won't only lead you to Manhattan. You'll discover many neighborhoods of Brooklyn and Queens, as well as Governors Island, Roosevelt Island, City Island, and north of Manhattan into the Hudson Valley.

I also wanted this piece to be a window onto New York for those who can't visit the city. I'm always looking to convey some piece or other of the metropolis' soul through my photos and character portraits.

Since we're talking about New Yorkers, people often ask me if they're nice. To tell you the truth, the reputation that precedes them (that they're rude, rushed and self-centered) is wrong. They're actually friendly and ready to help. They like confiding in strangers and will shamelessly tell you about the impossibility of finding a soul mate in New York, about the astronomical price of their rent, the suffocating August heat, the crumbling subway system, the crowded streets, the constant noise, the latest must-try restaurant or their neighborhood that's becoming dangerously gentrified.

There are many famous quotes about New York, but in my opinion, the one that best represents the city is from journalist

Alistair Cooke: "New York is the biggest collection of villages in the world." He's right: New York is kind of its own planet, a mosaic of cultures that live pushed up against each other in seldom-shaken harmony. In New York, difference is celebrated and social classes mix.

I love New York first and foremost for the snippets of conversations you can have with strangers you'll never see again, for smiles exchanged with a passenger on the opposite subway car, for the old man who removes his mittens to warm up your hands on the subway, for the cashier at the grocery store who calls you "My Love." From a bird's-eye view, New York is anxiety-inducing and intimidating, but it becomes familiar as you wander the grid of its streets. I love this city that drains your energy, and, in exchange, provides moments of happiness on every corner. This happiness is within reach for those who know how to catch it—those who know how to read the crowd.

"New York is the biggest collection of villages in the world."

MY TOPS

TOP 5 MY FAVORITE RESTAURANTS
1 **ABC Kitchen** [35 E 18th St]
2 **Indochine** [430 Lafayette St]
3 **Bar Pitti** [268 6th Ave]
4 **Terra** [222 W Broadway]
5 **Cafe Mogador** [101 St. Marks Pl; 133 Wythe Ave, Brooklyn]

TOP 5 THE BEST PIZZA
1 **Co.** [230 9th Ave]
2 **Lucali** [575 Henry St, Brooklyn]
3 **Paulie Gee's** [60 Greenpoint Ave, Brooklyn]
4 **Roberta's** [261 Moore St, Brooklyn]
5 **Kesté** [271 Bleecker St]
   Honorable mention: Don Antonio [309 W 50th St] **and Rubirosa** [235 Mulberry St]

TOP 5 THE BEST HAMBURGERS
1 **Minetta Tavern** [113 Macdougal St]
2 **Brindle Room** [227 E 10th St]
3 **Corner Bistro** [331 W 4th St]
4 **Burger Joint, in Le Parker Meridien Hotel** [119 W 56th St]
5 **Peter Luger** [178 Broadway, Brooklyn]

TOP 10 THE BEST CAFES
1 **La Colombe** [319 Church St]
2 **Laughing Man** [184 Duane St]
3 **Toby's Estate** [125 N 6th St, Brooklyn]
4 **Abraço Espresso** [86 E 7th St]
5 **Ground Support** [399 W Broadway]
6 **Brooklyn Roasting Company** [25 Jay St, Brooklyn]
7 **Ninth Street Espresso** [341 E 10th St]
8 **Gimme Coffee** [228 Mott St]
9 **Café Grumpy** [224 W 20th St]
10 **Stumptown** [30 W 8th St and 18 W 29th St]

207   223

TOP 10   ROOFTOP BARS

1 **The Ides**, at the top of the Wythe Hotel, in Williamsburg, with a beautiful view of Manhattan, perfect for watching the sunset [80 Wythe Ave, Brooklyn]
2 **Le Bain**, terrace on the roof of the Standard Hotel in the Meatpacking District with retro furniture and kiosque of fine pancakes [848 Washington St]
3 **Gallow Green**, garden with antique furniture on the roof of the McKittrick Hotel in Chelsea. Also open on the weekend for brunch [542 W 27th St]
4 **Refinery Rooftop**, bar in the fashion district with a view of the Empire State Building [63 W 38th St]
5 **Gramercy Park Hotel**, green terrace on the roof of the hotel, with a view of the Chrysler Building [2 Lexington Ave]
6 **The Roof**, in the Viceroy Hotel, luxurious bar set in a nautical style. There is a good view of Central Park from the terrace [124 W 57th St]
7 **The Press Lounge** of the Ink48 Hotel, large terrace with a view of the Hudson River and Midtown [653 11th Ave]
8 **Pod 39 Hotel**, fabulous terrace with red-bricked arches and a view of Midtown [145 E 39th St]
9 **Birreria**, brasserie on the roof of the Eataly Market with a view of the Flatiron Building [200 5th Ave]
10 **Northern Territory**, Australian restaurant with a rooftop terrace and a view of Manhattan and the Empire State Building [12 Franklin St, Brooklyn]

TOP 10   THE NICEST STREETS

1 **Pomander Walk**, Upper West Side
2 **Warren Place Mews**, Cobble Hill
3 **Grace Court Alley**, Brooklyn Heights
4 **Love Lane Mews**, Brooklyn Heights
5 **Sylvan Terrace**, Washington Heights
6 **Washington Mews**, Greenwich Village
7 **Grove Court**, West Village
8 **MacDougal Alley**, Greenwich Village
9 **Patchin Place**, Greenwich Village
10 **Block Beautiful** [E 19th St, between 3rd Ave and Irving Pl], Gramercy

TOP 20 BOUTIQUE HOTELS

1   **Greenwich Hotel**, in TriBeCa (Robert De Niro's hotel with an inner courtyard and an underground swimming pool)
2   **Gramercy Park Hotel,** in Gramercy (luxurious hotel with a rooftop garden)
3   **Crosby Street Hotel,** in SoHo (hotel with a tearoom adorned with living art)
4   **The NoMad Hotel,** in the NoMad neighborhood (Parisian-style hotel with a world-class restaurant)
5   **The Marlton Hotel,** in Greenwich Village (historic Parisian-style building and former haunt of artists)
6   **Ace Hotel,** in the NoMad neighborhood (hip hotel for trendy youth)
7   **Wythe Hotel,** Williamsburg, Brooklyn (hotel with a trendy rooftop bar, a restaurant and bunk beds for musicians)
8   **The Bowery Hotel,** in NoHo (trendy hotel frequented by the stars)
9   **The Jane,** in West Village (historic building on the banks of the Hudson, with small, charming rooms)
10 **The High Line Hotel,** in Chelsea (in an old seminary near High Line Park)
11 **The Mercer,** in SoHo (in the heart of the action, the hotel that the stars prefer)
12 **The Broome,** in SoHo (rooms looking over an inner courtyard)
13 **The Standard Hotel,** in East Village (a number of dining rooms, terraces and a panoramic view of New York)
14 **The Standard Hotel,** in the Meatpacking District (the destination for those in the fashion industry, in a Soviet-style tower with bay windows overlooking High Line Park)
15 **The Ludlow,** in the Lower East Side (many rooms with private terraces)
16 **Smyth Hotel,** in TriBeCa (ideally located, chic and comfortable, with a great lounge and bar)
17 **Hotel Hugo,** in Soho (design hotel near the Hudson River, away from tourist areas)
18 **Martha Washington Hotel,** in the NoMad neighborhood (built in 1903 and restored in 2014, this historic hotel was once reserved for women only)
19 **Madison Square Park,** (housed in the Metropolitan Life Insurance Company clock tower, built in 1909)
20 **Refinery Hotel,** in the Garment District (located in the fashion district, the hotel was once a hat factory)

TOP 10   AFFORDABLE AND WELL-LOCATED HOTELS

1   **The Sheraton,** in TriBeCa (renovated hotel, rooftop terrace with a view of Manhattan and continental breakfast included)

2   **The Hudson,** in Midtown, near Central Park (the rooms are small, but the prices range from $100 to $300. Decor by designer Philippe Starck)

3   **The NYLO,** in the Upper West Side (some rooms have private balconies, and the view of Central Park from the 16th-story terrace is spectacular)

4   **The Duane Street Hotel,** in TriBeCa (small, but functional rooms, on one of the prettiest streets in the neighborhood)

5   **The Gershwin Hotel,** in the NoMad neighborhood (eccentric hotel, the rooms cost an average of $200, WiFi)

6   **Pod 39 Hotel and Pod 51 Hotel,** in Midtown, close to Grand Central Station, the Empire State Building and Times Square (tiny, but functional rooms, starting at $200 a night, free WiFi)

7   **Holiday Inn,** in the heart of SoHo (good location, rooms average $189 a night)

8   **La Quinta Inn Manhattan** (just steps away from the Empire State Building, renovated and rooms about $219 a night)

9   **Chelsea Lodge** (bed and breakfast with charming decor in an old brownstone)

10 **YMCA West Side** (very affordable, youth hostel style, just steps from Central Park)

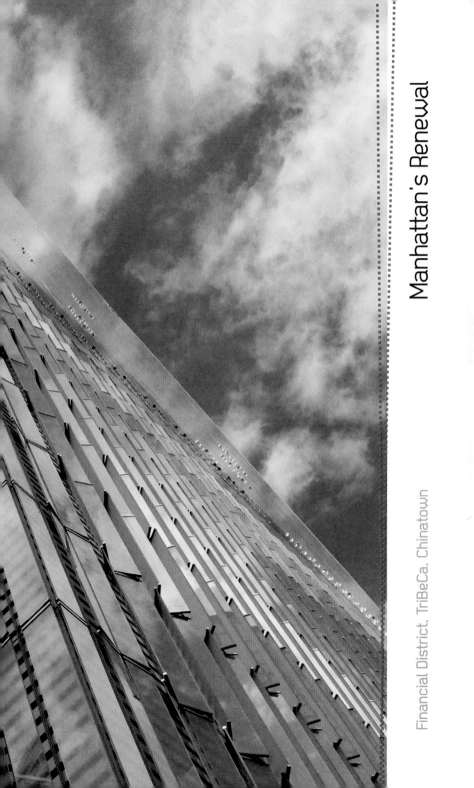

Manhattan's Renewal

Financial District, TriBeCa, Chinatown

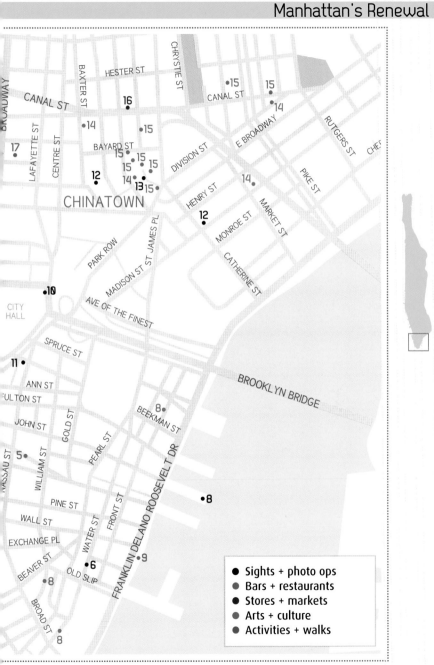

CHRYSTIE ST

HESTER ST

BAXTER ST

BROADWAY

CANAL ST

•15
CANAL ST

15

•14

LAFAYETTE ST

CENTRE ST

•14

•15

RUTGERS ST

E BROADWAY

CHE

17
•

16
•

BAYARD ST

DIVISION ST

15
•
12
•

15
•
14 •

15
15
•
13 15•

PIKE ST

HENRY ST

14
•

CHINATOWN

PARK ROW

MADISON ST

ST JAMES PL

MONROE ST

MARKET ST

12
•

CATHERINE ST

AVE OF THE FINEST

•10

CITY
HALL

SPRUCE ST

11 •

ANN ST

FULTON ST

BROOKLYN BRIDGE

JOHN ST

GOLD ST

8•

BEEKMAN ST

PEARL ST

NASSAU ST

5 •

WILLIAM ST

FRANKLIN DELANO ROOSEVELT DR

PINE ST

FRONT ST

•8

WALL ST

WATER ST

EXCHANGE PL

BEAVER ST

•6

OLD SLIP

•9

•8

BROAD ST

8

- ● Sights + photo ops
- ● Bars + restaurants
- ● Stores + markets
- ● Arts + culture
- ● Activities + walks

The Street Teacher

1 Every day for the past 14 years, **Harry John Roland** has gone to the site of the World Trade Center. Rain or snow, he stands at the corner of Liberty and Greenwich with a single purpose: to make sure we never forget. He can often be seen cleaning and polishing the bronze Memorial Wall dedicated to the firefighters who died on 9/11, located at the famous fire station across from Ground Zero. New Yorkers know him as Harry History, and the workers at the site have adopted him. "They've given me a tour of the site a few times. They keep me updated on new developments."

Now in his sixties, Harry is a bona fide history buff and—above all—a walking encyclopedia when it comes to the Twin Towers. Since the attacks of September 11, 2001, the towers have become an obsession for him.

All day, tourists passing by hear him chant his familiar refrain: "History, don't let it be a mystery! How many buildings used to be here? Don't say two 'cause that's not true." Most tourists have no idea. Over the years, the details have faded from the collective memory. Harry answers his own question: "There were seven." He meticulously recounts the story of the attacks, and addresses questions to his audience: "How many firefighters died that day, ma'am?" "Three hundred and forty-three," a tourist replies. "That's right," responds Mr. Roland, who lives off of tips from people walking by.

September 11 Memorial and Museum

2 This is not the kind of place where New Yorkers like to linger, but a visit here is necessary even if it is just to pay tribute at the twin fountains to the 2,983 people who lost their lives on September 11, 2001.

The **National 9/11 Memorial** features two enormous pools, each about 4,000 square meters (one acre) in size, set within the footprints of the Twin Towers and fed by 10-meter, (30-foot) high waterfalls that mute the sounds of the city. The names of the 2,983 victims are inscribed in bronze around the twin memorial pools.

Michael Arad, the Israeli-American architect who worked eight years on this massive project, told me that the biggest challenge was to create not only a sacred place that would suit the families but also a public space that New Yorkers would want to call their own.

The twin memorial pools featuring the largest fountains in North America were designed in Canada by Ontario sculptor and architect Dan Euser. They run off 197,000 liters (52,000 gallons) of recycled water per minute, 365 days of the year.

The **National September 11 Memorial Museum** is located 21 meters (70 feet) under the **National September 11 Memorial.** The exhibition space displays 10,000 artifacts including the famous Ground Zero cross, the Survivors' Staircase, nearly 23,000 images of the events, 500 hours of film and videos and 1,970 oral testimonies to the victims. This is an overwhelming experience.

The **One World Observatory** with the fastest elevators in the world and its multimedia observation platform on the 100th floor of the new One World Trade Center tower has been open to the public since 2015.

The Twin Towers Tightrope Walker

3 It's hard to believe that when they were first built in the 1970s, New Yorkers were less than thrilled about the Twin Towers—they found them to be too "utilitarian." Nevertheless, little more than a year after the inauguration of the **World Trade Center** in 1973, Frenchman **Philippe Petit** pulled off what some have called "the artistic crime of the century" ("crime" because these types of stunts are illegal). On August 7, 1974, he performed a high-wire walk between the two towers. The performance lasted 45 minutes, and the story spread around the world.

The extent of his feat is difficult to fathom—particularly since the 9/11 attacks. In preparation for his high-wire walk 417 meters (1,368 feet) above the streets of Manhattan, Petit had to thwart security to transport a 200-kilogram (441-pound) steel cable and an eight-meter (26-foot) long bar to the 104th floor of the South Tower.

"Today, they would take me down on the spot," Philippe Petit told me during an interview in a Brooklyn warehouse, where people train for climbing and the circus arts. In 1968, while waiting for a dental appointment, the young Philippe came upon a magazine containing pictures of the World Trade Center, then under construction. From that moment on, he was obsessed with the Twin Towers and began collecting everything relating to them.

Thereafter, Petit visited New York several times to study the towers, how much they swayed at the top and the daily routines of the people who worked there. To finance the operation, he borrowed $20,000 from friends, repaying them several years later. To get the steel cable from one tower to the other, Petit and his accomplices used a bow and arrow. The arrow was attached to a fishing line, which was attached to bigger and bigger ropes, until they were able to string the steel cable between the two towers.

Finally, just after 7 a.m. on August 7, 1974, Philippe Petit began his performance, walking the length of the 43-meter (141-foot) long wire a total of eight times. Half a kilometer (1,400 feet) below, bewildered bystanders watched in awe.

This experience sealed the Frenchman's love for New York forever. He now lives on a farm north of the city, and has installed a tightrope in his garden, where he practices for three hours each day. He has also written 10 novels and gives lectures on creativity around the world.

I took a chance and broached the delicate subject of September 11, 2001. "I don't talk about it much," he said. "I was at the farm that day and my friends called to tell me, since I don't have a television. It's hard to describe the feeling that came over me; I had such a personal attachment to those towers." He knew them by heart. So much so that, after his arrest, the New York Police Department asked for his advice on how to improve site security.

Forty years later, he sometimes doubts whether he really accomplished such a miraculous feat. "I used to return to the towers, to lie down on the roof and relive that day in 1974. The towers are no longer there, but they are still in me."

In 2008, James Marsh released *Man on Wire*, a documentary film that recounts in great detail the organizing that went into what Petit called the "coup" in 1974. Ever since I met him, I have been haunted by this fearless man who does not take no for an answer.

The Food Truck Business

4 One of the biggest **food truck** rallies is located just opposite Zuccotti Park, home of the Occupy Wall Street movement at Broadway and Cedar Streets. At noon, Wall Street bankers flock into the square for a quick meal. This is one of the rare places where you can still get coffee in the iconic Anthora paper coffee cup, the same one that has been seen in all the movies with the phrase *"we are happy to serve you"* written on the side. Street—vendors and delis have been using these famous paper cups for over 50 years. Leslie Buck, the designer of this city icon who died in 2010, decided to pay homage to the Greeks who owned most of the delis at the time, by using the Greek vase motif and the blue and white colors of the Greek flag in his design for the cup. In New York the Anthora cup is as famous as the Statue of Liberty and can even be found in the Metropolitan Museum of Art (MoMa). You can buy a ceramic version in the SoHo MoMa boutique [81 Spring St] and in Midtown [44 West 33rd St]. I buy them as gifts for all my friends.

Walking on Gold

5 The typical immigrant landing in New York in the 19th century used to say that he had come to New York because he had heard that the streets were paved in gold. This may not be the case today, but under New York's sidewalks there is said to be more gold than anywhere else in the world. You can confirm this by visiting the **Federal Reserve Bank** in the Financial District. The free guided tour gives you access to the gold vault, which is five floors underground and where it is said that almost 7,000 tons of gold bullion or the equivalent of several hundred billion dollars are stored. This is more than at Fort Knox. Reservations are necessary for this visit at: newyorkfed.org (Museum and Gold Vault Tour) Photos are not permitted [44 Maiden Lane].

A 19ᵗʰ-Century Candy Store

6 My favorite building on Wall Street is the tower at 77 Water Street. From a distance it looks like an ordinary office tower but as you approach the main lobby you can see a 19ᵗʰ-century candy store on the left. Right out front of the building, there are also several contemporary sculptures and some retro-futuristic payphones. Since 1969, an old rusty World War I fighter plane has been sitting on an Astroturf runway positioned on the rooftop. Unfortunately the only way to get a glimpse of it is from the top of neighboring buildings, such as the terrace of the Andaz Hotel just next door.

Phentex Artwork by Olek

7 If you run into any street furniture in south Manhattan covered with pink or mauve Phentex yarn it will be artist **Olek**'s artwork. For the last few years it has been impossible to wander about New York without seeing a bicycle or a stroller covered in crochet. The artist, Agata Oleksiak, born in a small industrial Polish village, has been living in New York for nearly 15 years and has a workshop in the Financial District. She began to crochet because it was the cheapest way to develop her artistic talent and in 2010, became a household name when she covered Arturo di Modica's bronze Wall Street Bull sculpture with crochet.

South Street Seaport

8 There is another side to the South Street Seaport. Considered to be the Times Square of south Manhattan, New Yorkers avoid this area. Nevertheless there are several authentic spots such as **Luke's Lobster**, a small restaurant where you can get lobster rolls for $15 a piece [26 South William St] and **The Dead Rabbit**, an Irish pub [30 Water St] where you can choose from an impressive list of 72 cocktails in an 1850s-inspired decor. For a good cup of coffee I go to **Jack's Coffee** [222 Front St].

I also like to go to revamped **Pier 15** where there is a two-level observation deck with a few benches and a spectacular view on the **East River** and the Brooklyn Bridge [at the corner of South and Fletcher St].

At sunset a walk along the East River is a must. This is the ideal place for taking pictures of the famous Brooklyn and Manhattan bridges as well as for striking up a conversation with a few fishermen.

Taking the IKEA Ferry to Brooklyn

9 Most New Yorkers don't have cars and so they go to IKEA by boat. If you feel like visiting Brooklyn while wandering around the South Street Seaport you can take the **New York Water Taxi**'s IKEA Express shuttle service directly to Red Hook. It's the fastest way to get to this booming area. (See reasons #253 and #255 to #257). The shuttle, leaving from Wall Street's Pier 11, is free on the weekends but costs $5.00 during the week. On the return trip you'll be accompanied by customers carrying BILLY bookcases and POANG Chairs.

The Secret Subway Station

10 There is a subway station under New York's city hall that has been abandoned since 1945 because it couldn't take the longer trains. To see it, take Line 6 southbound and stay on the train after the Brooklyn Bridge–City Hall stop, which is the last one. The subway then loops around and goes past the secret station. You can see it through the windows and it is like discovering New York in another era. This architectural marvel with its arched ceiling, mosaics, stained glass windows and chandeliers is reminiscent of the Moscow subway stations. The **New York Transit Museum** in Brooklyn occasionally organizes guided tours of this station.

The Abandoned Palace

11 Just a stone's throw from New York's city hall is a building frozen in time that had been unknown to the public until just recently. In 1883, Eugene Kelly, an Irish immigrant and prosperous businessman built a nine-story building that he called **Temple Court**. Kelly invested $400,000 in the construction of this gem of terra cotta, wood paneling, mosaics and cast iron. A skylight crowning the atrium is the masterpiece of this building. One of the largest vaults in the city is in the basement. At the time of writing this, Temple Court is closed to the public and plans are underway to convert it into a boutique hotel with 287 rooms and two high-end restaurants. The Beekman Hotel is scheduled to open in 2016 [5 Beekman St; thebeekman.com].

The **Woolworth Building** on the other side of City Hall Park is another New York gem. Classified as a historical monument in 1966, the lobby has been closed to the public until recently. Guided tours are now available [233 Broadway; woolworthtours.com].

Real Chinatown

12 When I feel like like shaking things off and falling in love with New York again I head to **Chinatown**. The "real" Chinatown is located on the Lower East Side, east of the Bowery and far away from Canal Street with its dealers selling fake goods.

I like looking at the stores on Madison Street and the locals doing Tai Chi at Columbus Park [Mulberry and Bayard St]. If you have seen Martin Scorsese's movie *Gangs of New York*, you will be interested to know that this is where the famous Five Points District was filmed.

An Underground Restaurant and a Former Opium Den

14 **Bacaro**, an Italian restaurant located in the center of Chinatown is one of the best-kept secrets in the area. I often go there and have celebrated several birthdays in this place. The big wooden tables are ideal for large groups and the fact that it is underground gives you the impression that you're dining in a wine cellar [136 Division St].

For an evening of old New York atmosphere I go to **Forlini's** restaurant, and sample simple Italian American food. The decor is over-the-top kitsch with pink leather booths and oil paintings, but that's what gives it its charm. Friday evenings, local legend Angelo Ruggiero sings Frank Sinatra's old hits and the customers get up and dance between the tables. Try the cheese ravioli or the eggplant Parmesan, [93 Baxter St].

After dinner I usually head to **Mr. Fong's** bar [40 Market St] where they serve Asian-inspired cocktails or **Apotheke**, which is a former opium den. The barmen here are dressed in apothecary outfits and the cocktails are said to be medicinal and even aphrodisiacal. Most of the alcoholic drinks have been infused with herbs. I recommend Kale in Comparison. The bar is under the **Gold Flower Restaurant** sign [9 Doyers St].

Chinatown's Secret Tunnel

13 My favorite streets in this area are Pell and Doyers. They look like movie sets. **Doyers Street**, a dogleg alley less than 110 yards long, was known at the beginning of the last century as "The Bloody Angle" because several murders had taken place there. This secret tunnel, which still exists and has a few businesses in it, enabled some of the victims and murderers to escape. The entrance is at 7-8 Chatham Square. Unfortunately, in 2015, half of the tunnel was converted into the nightlife venue Chinese Tuxedo.

15A

Eating Well on the Cheap

15 Chinatown is one of the few areas of New York where you can eat like a king for just a few dollars. **Nom Wah Tea Parlor** (A) is a place I love. It opened in 1927 and is one of the oldest restaurants in the area. The decor has remained the same since the 1950s. Today's owner, a former Wall Street stockbroker, took over the business from his uncle [13 Doyers St].

Prosperity Dumpling is a tiny hole-in-the-wall, but they serve excellent dumplings. The items on the menu are a mere $2.00 [46 Eldridge St]. **Joe's Shanghai** is the restaurant that claims to have invented dumpling soup. It is open late and is always crowded [9 Pell St].

Tasty Hand-Pulled Noodles [1 Doyers St] and **Xi'an Famous Foods** [67 Bayard St] are my favorite places for fresh noodles.

If you like seafood, **Oriental Garden** is the place where many chefs go on their day off. There is an aquarium from which you can choose your own crab. [14 Elizabeth St].

For ice cream, **The Original Chinatown Ice Cream Factory** has almost 30 original flavors, including lychee, sesame, avocado, green tea and red bean [65 Bayard St].

For a healthy meal, **Dimes** (B) is the best bet in the area. The tiny Californian-style restaurant is known for its salads, vegetable dishes and bowls of acai and pollen [49 Canal St].

A $15 Blow-Dry

16

Anyone who knows anything about anything knows that New York is a humid city and that it is useless to pay $50 in a midtown salon for a blow-dry. Most Chinatown salons charge $15 for a cut and blow-dry, which includes a long massage, two shampoos, a blow-dry and flat-iron finish. I am a regular customer at **Mian Tian Sing Hair Salon**. Once ensconced in the chair, it's an hour and a half of lost in translation for me as no one speaks English, the radio blares out Chinese pop music and the magazines are all in Mandarin. Reservations are not necessary and you can always get in [170 Canal St, 2nd floor].

The Elevator Museum

17

Mmuseumm is the smallest museum in New York. Located in an elevator shaft in the middle of a small street in TriBeCa, bordering Chinatown, it measures scarcely five square meters (54 square feet). Museum exhibits display strange everyday objects and artifacts from around the world, which change seasonally. You might enjoy the collection of coffee cup lids or homemade gas masks or objects found in patients' bodies by a Massachusetts doctor. Don't miss the museum's new addition, **Mmuseumm2**. It's located on the same small street. [Cortland Alley, between Franklin and White St].

Canteens in TriBeCa

18

Terra Winebar is my favorite restaurant in TriBeCa. It is also one of the rare places in the area where you can eat well without breaking the bank. There is a wide selection of small Italian dishes and the terrace is very pleasant during the summer [222 West Broadway].

I also like the French bistro **Racines** [94 Chambers St] because of its excellent wine list. Marseille chef Frédéric Duca is assisted in the kitchen by Canadian Emily Campeau—another reason to go there.

Sole di Capri serves authentic Italian food at low prices. Don't be put off by the somewhat tacky decor; Italians are regular customers in this small unpretentious restaurant. The owner, Graziano Lembo from Capri, uses his mother's recipes with ingredients imported from Italy. (165 Church St).

For important occasions, I like chef Andrew Carmellini's Italian restaurant **Locanda Verde** in the Greenwich Hotel. This place is very popular at noon and in the evening so it is a good idea to reserve in advance [377 Greenwich St]. If you can't get in here, Carmellini has another restaurant in the area, **Little Park** (A) [85 West Broadway].

Other good eateries on Greenwich Street are **Estancia 460**, an Argentinian bistro that has Italian and Spanish culinary influences [460 Greenwich St], and next to it **The Greek** [458 Greenwich St]. These two places have small street-side terraces.

China Blue, tucked away in an obscure corner of TriBeCa, is a hidden treasure. It serves excellent dim sum in a setting reminiscent of 1930s Shanghai [135 Watts St].

When taking the subway, always have your MetroCard in hand when you approach the turnstiles. Swipe the pass as you would a credit card: neither too slowly nor too quickly. It's an art that I have yet to master. #onlyinNY

Brunchtime in TriBeCa

19 **Bubby's** (A) is by far the most popular place for lavish brunches. Their specialties are pies and crepes [120 Hudson St]. John F. Kennedy Jr. and Carolyn Bessette used to go there when they lived in a loft on the ninth floor in a building very close by [20 Moore St].

At noon I really like **Mulberry and Vine**, which has a salad bar with health-food dishes [73 Warren St].

For a fabulous almond croissant go to **Arcade Bakery** (B) set up in a hallway of the office building at 220 Church Street. Roger Gural, the baker is well known in the United States. He studied at Bouchon and the French Laundry in California. He also cooks delicious individual pizzas on order.

My Area

20 **TriBeCa**, which gets its name from the first letters of the words "**Tri**angle **Be**low **Ca**nal Street," is my adopted home-turf. I like this area because of its cobblestone streets, small independent boutiques, more relaxed pace of life and mainly because there are very few tourists. There are many families living in TriBeCa and certain restaurants even have designated areas for strollers.

Today this former industrial zone is south Manhattan's bourgeois area. Several noted musicians live there including Jay-Z, Beyoncé and Taylor Swift. Robert De Niro owns several buildings in the area, one of which houses the sushi restaurant Nobu and the fabulous Greenwich Hotel, which is somewhat the equivalent of Chateau Marmont in Los Angeles. Rooms are sophisticated, and bathrooms come with Moroccan tile and Italian marble. Drop in to check out the hall and back garden. In the basement, there is also a spa that is open to the public.

The Ghostbusters' Fire Station

21 **Hook & Ladder 8** is the iconic fire station featured in the movie *Ghostbusters*. Inside you can see the original plastic sign of the ghost that hung over the doorway in the 1984 film. The fire station is still operational today, but it was severely affected by the 9/11 attacks when several of its crew lost their lives. If the door is open, the firefighters will take pride in showing you their collection of old melted telephones saved from charred houses through the years [44 North Moore St].

22A 24

TriBeCa Landmarks

22

In spite of the city's constant renewal, certain institutions manage to survive the passage of time without losing their customers, as in the case of **The Odeon**. When the restaurant opened in 1980, this part of the city was a no man's land but it soon became the trendy place for people working in the fashion industry and local stars such as Andy Warhol. Several films were shot here and this is where Carrie Bradshaw's favorite cocktail, the celebrated Cosmopolitan, is said to have originated [145 West Broadway].

Just next to it is **The Square Diner** (A), one of New York's authentic diners. Slide onto one of the leather booths and pretend you are in the Martin Scorsese film *After Hours* [33 Leonard St].

22A

Flat Whites the Way Hugh Jackman Likes Them

23

Laughing Man (A) is a coffee shop located on Duane Street, the most beautiful street in TriBeCa. You might run into Hugh Jackman here as he is the owner. Order a Flat White like he does. It's an Australian cappuccino. **Bikini Bar** cafe, with its crazy Hawaiian surfing decor, including restored bamboo furniture, serves organic iced coffee. It is on the next corner [148 Duane Street].

A Gastronomic Experience in TriBeCa

24

Chef David Bouley and the Japanese Tsuji Culinary Institute jointly own the relatively unknown restaurant **Brushstroke**, located in a quiet part of TriBeCa. It was there that I had one of the most memorable gastronomic experiences since arriving in New York. The tasting menu ($85-$135 without alcohol) changes seasonally. There is also an excellent sushi bar just beside the dining room [3 Hudson St]. For a less expensive gastronomic experience in a more relaxed

atmosphere, the Austrian restaurant Bâtard has a four-course menu for $82. In 2015, Bâtard was awarded Best New Restaurant in America by the James Beard Foundation [239 West Broadway].

Barhopping in TriBeCa

25 **Brandy Library** (A) looks like a library for a billionaire. It's a place where you can choose from a wide selection of cognacs or the 100 cocktail options in a plush old New York atmosphere [25 North Moore].

Smith & Mills (B) is a bar/restaurant, in a converted carriage house, serves a few dishes and is an excellent spot for a first date [71 N Moore].

With his lounge **Baby Grand**, New York's nightlife maestro and DJ Paul Sevigny (brother of Chloë) has tried to create one of the most flamboyant bars in New York. Floral wallpaper, pictures of palm trees, zebra armchairs and enormous bouquets of flowers make up the decor. Baby Grand is located in the **Roxy Hotel** [2 Avenue of the Americas].

The Warren 77 sports tavern looks like a hockey dressing room, which makes it a great place to watch your favorite team [77 Warren St].

An empty subway car is empty for a good reason. Don't get on. Instead, hop onto another car. #onlyinNY

New York's Most Fun Store

26 All of you who follow me on Instagram will recognize this store as I take a picture of it at least once a week. Every day, **Balloon Saloon**'s owner sets up a big bunch of balloons and numerous inflated figures in front of her store. Inside she sells hundreds of balloons, including ones that sing, others that are heart- and star-shaped, round ones, and even cats and dogs—as well as decorative items and many humorous gags. This is the place for a unique gift [133 West Broadway].

27 B

Find a Rare Item

27

Steven Alan is a chain of stores with unusual items from up-and-coming designers. For clothing, shoes, jewelry and housewares there are two locations in TriBeCa [103 and 158 Franklin St].

For menswear, it is worth checking out the **J.Crew** store (A) [235 West Broadway] located in a former tavern built in 1825. J.Crew also has another store that does custom-made suits and accessories, **The Ludlow Shop** [50 Hudson St].

All the products (watches, bicycles and leather goods, including dog beds, phone cases, bracelets, wallets and bags) at **Shinola** are made in Detroit. Stop for a few minutes in the charming cafe that is at the entrance to the store [177 Franklin St].

Philip Williams (B) has been selling vintage posters under his own name, Philip Williams Posters, for more than 40 years in a huge loft that is really a poster museum.

27 A

There are over 2,500 posters in his collection of animals, films, travel, food and fashion. He even has several that date back to the art deco era. [122 Chambers St].

An Arabian Nights Water Spa

28

Aire Ancient Baths with its Moroccan lanterns, brick walls and numerous thermal baths is a unique spot in TriBeCa. The underground spa boasts waterfalls and six pools ranging from 9°C (46°F) to 39°C (102°F). Treatments include aromatherapy and massage therapy. A great idea for Valentine gifts from $75 [88 Franklin St].

A Surprising Memorial

29

The **Irish Hunger Memorial**, located at Vesey Street and North End Avenue, is an important memorial dedicated to raising awareness about the hundreds of thousands of Irish who, between 1845 and 1852, fled the Irish Potato Famine and arrived in New York. The memorial includes an abandoned stone cottage and a rural Irish landscape set on an elevated platform. Visitors can stroll along the pathways and through the tall grass.

29

Wandering the Hudson River

30

The **Downtown Boathouse** is an all-volunteer nonprofit organization that offers 20-minute kayak access. You can paddle down a part of the Hudson River, protected from big boats and water currents. It is one of the rare activities in the city that is still free. Three locations: **Pier 26**, just north of North Moore Street; **Pier 96** at 56th Street; and another one at 72nd Street.

The bike path on the west side of Manhattan is a haven for sports enthusiasts. It is like another Central Park for those who live on the West Side. There are several basketball, volleyball and tennis courts; and most of the piers have outdoor playgrounds for children. I particularly like the Mini Golf at Pier 25 ($5 for adults and $4 for children 13 and under).

The lawns of **Nelson A. Rockefeller Park** in Battery Park City are the ideal place for a picnic. Even outdoor billiard tables are available. And there are four places nearby for food: **Whole Foods** [270 Greenwich St]; the burger stand **Shake Shack** [215 Murray St]; the bakery **Le Pain Quotidien** [2 River Terrace] and **Le District**, a big French market [225 Brookfield Pl]. Battery Park City sprung to life in the 1970s. It was built as an annex to Manhattan when more than 917,000 cubic meters (1.2 million cubic yards) of soil and rock excavated during the construction of the World Trade Center and other construction projects became available.

31A

31B

Cocktails and Oysters on a Schooner

31 **Grand Banks** (A) is a bar and restaurant on the deck of the *Sherman Zwicker,* a historic fishing vessel. The schooner, built in Nova Scotia in 1942, has been anchored at the Hudson River's Pier 25, North Moore Street, in TriBeCa, since 2014. At 43 meters (142 feet), it is the biggest wooden vessel in New York and its hold has been transformed into a small maritime museum. Grand Banks is a place where they serve several varieties of oysters and small dishes and an ideal venue for a drink at the end of the day.

A little farther south at North Cove Marina near the World Financial Center, the company **Manhattan by Sail** offers two-hour tours of the Hudson River on a huge schooner. Other kinds of cruises are available by day and by night. The *Clipper City* (B) tall ship, the bigger of the two boats, has a bar on board and is a venue for jazz concerts [manhattanbysail.com].

Gastronomic Pleasures and the Nightlife

SoHo, Nolita, Lower East Side

SoHo, Nolita, Lower East Side

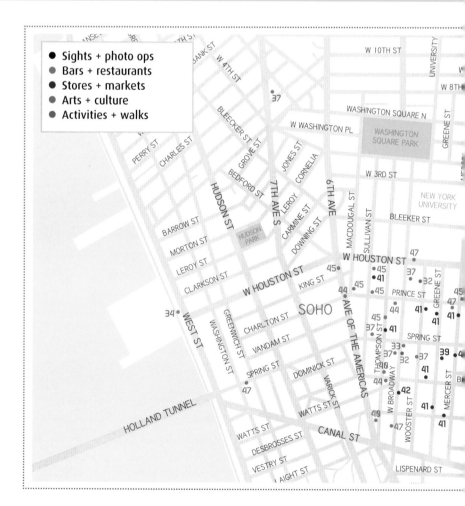

- ● Sights + photo ops
- ● Bars + restaurants
- ● Stores + markets
- ● Arts + culture
- ● Activities + walks

Gastronomic Pleasures and the Nightlife

The Art Gallery from Another Era

32

From the beginning of the 1970s to the end of the 1980s, **SoHo** was New York's artistic neighborhood. Artists could rent huge industrial lofts at ridiculously low prices, but once designer boutiques started opening, rents were driven up. The majority of galleries are now farther north, in Chelsea. There are still a few unexpected spots, like this gallery that has featured the same exhibit since 1979, **The Broken Kilometer**. It's a golden, kilometer-long brass rod that's been cut into 500 bars that are laid out in five rows on the wooden floor. The installation by Walter De Maria is unique, especially in an area where each square foot is worth its weight in gold. It's one of the last non-commercial spaces in SoHo. [393 W Broadway].

A stone's throw away, you can visit another permanent exhibit—**The New York Earth Room**—by the same artist. This 334-square-meter (3,600-square-foot) loft is filled with 140 tons of black soil, and the place has not changed since 1977 [141 Wooster St]. Both exhibits are free, but photography is not allowed.

34

The Artists' Cafe

33

Ground Support is a hit with regulars, including the neighborhood's residents, as well as many artists, authors and intellectuals. That's where I happened to meet director Paul Haggis who was working on a movie script, as well as Malcolm Gladwell who was writing an article with such concentration that made it seem as if he was the last man on Earth. Steven, the owner, is a bike lover, and his establishment is full of cycling magazines and issues of *National Geographic*. He makes delicious panini on-site. There are two benches on the sidewalk in front of the cafe, and I truly believe it to be one of the best spots to people-watch in New York. [399 W Broadway].

Swing from a Trapeze like Carrie

34

There is a trapeze school on Houston Street, on a bank of the Hudson River, where you can take a class in the evening at sunset ($70 for two hours). The school is located on the roof of a building with a breathtaking view of the Statue of Liberty. It became very popular after an episode of *Sex and the City* in which Carrie Bradshaw took a trapeze class for her column [Pier 40, Hudson River Park; newyork.trapezeschool.com].

Around the World in a Bookstore

35 I love browsing at **McNally-Jackson**, one of the few independent bookstores left in New York. The Canadian owner, Sarah McNally, encourages customers to read on the spot. Books and authors are categorized by country of origin, and her magazine section is one of the most varied in town. This bookstore also has an amazing machine that allows people to print a paperback book from a selection of four million works in just a few minutes [52 Prince St]. Two annexes set up shop on Mulberry Street, just a few feet away. **McNally Jackson Store** sells great office supplies, and **Picture Room** showcases a selection of prints and rare posters [234 and 236 Mulberry St].

Balthazar's Steak Frites

36 Here's the perfect place for those who are visiting New York for the first time. **Balthazar** is a Parisian-style *brasserie* inspired by the restaurant Bouillon Chartier in Paris. Founded in 1997, it is New York celebrity chef Keith McNally's most famous establishment. I prefer going on weeknights when there are fewer tourists, but the Sunday brunch is also a must. Order a mimosa, the pastry basket, onion soup, *niçoise* salad or *steak frites*, and take in this famous SoHo eatery's atmosphere. [80 Spring St].

36

The Dessert District

37

To get your hands on macarons you could find in Paris and savor them in a dining room worthy of Madame de Pompadour, head over to **Ladurée** (A) [398 W Broadway]. Two blocks away, you'll find a famous bakery by **Dominique Ansel**, the inventor of the cronut (a croissant-doughnut) and Cookie Shots [189 Spring St]. In their West Village location, **Dominique Ansel Kitchen**, all desserts are made fresh to order, in front of your eyes [137 7th Ave S]. For the best French toast in town, head to the popular brunch spot, **Sadelle's** [463 West Broadway]. **Ceci-Cela**, French pastry chef Laurent Dupal's counter, has been open for over 20 years. I recommend the almond croissant [55 Spring St]. **Momofuku Milk Bar** (B) serves up cereal milk soft-serve and the famous compost cookies [72 Wooster St].

Afternoon Tea Downtown

38

Crosby Street is considered to be New York's artsiest hotel. It has contemporary art pieces on each floor, so tour the lobby before taking a seat in the dining room. You can also have tea in the courtyard. They serve scones, delicious sandwiches, cupcakes and mini chocolate pies (about $35 per person for a meal). There are four chickens that live in a vegetable garden on the roof, and they are named after New York boroughs: Brooklyn, Queens, Bronx and Manhattan [79 Crosby St].

The Apartment Where Everything is for Sale

39 Located on the 3rd floor of a magnificent SoHo edifice built in 1872, **The Apartment by The Line** gives the initial impression that you've barged into a wealthy New Yorker's dwelling. It's rather a new retail concept imagined by stylist Vanessa Traina. Everything is for sale in this large loft, from bed to bedding, along with the drapes, light fixtures, bath products, clothes and even the photos on the walls [76 Greene St].

39

Shopping Musts

41 The list of good shops in this neighborhood is endless, but here are a few I often stop in at. For clothing and accessories, I go to **A.P.C** [131 Mercer St], **Alexander Wang** [103 Grand St], **Acne Studios** [33 Greene St], **Helmut Lang** [93 Mercer St], **TIBI** [120 Wooster St] and the Japanese brand **Tomorrowland**'s boutique [476 Broome St]. To find rare and vintage glasses, I try **Illesteva** [49 Prince St] or **Silver Lining** [92 Thompson St], and nice photography books can be found at **Taschen** [107 Greene St].

For men, **Palmer Trading Company** (A) has a great selection of American-made clothing, as well as many vintage pieces [137 Sullivan St]. For men's jewelry and accessories, have a look at the **Miansai** boutique [33 Crosby St]. Next door, you can step into **Saturdays**, a surf shop right in the heart of SoHo. There, you'll find accessories, clothing and books. In the summertime, stay a while drinking coffee in the lovely backyard garden [31 Crosby St].

Rooftop Terraces

40 **Jimmy**, the **James Hotel**'s rooftop bar [15 Thompson St], provides a 360-degree view of the skyline and the opportunity (a rare one in Manhattan) to have a poolside drink. **A60**, the **60 Thompson** hotel's rooftop patio, also has a spectacular view of SoHo. The vibe is more intimate, and bands play live music on Sundays [60 Thompson St].

41A

Vintage Treasures

42 To find unique vintage clothing, **What Goes Around Comes Around** is *the* go-to secondhand shop for New York stylists. Since 1993, co-owners Gerard Maione and Seth Weisser have collected rare pieces. They specialize in rock clothing from the 1960s, along with many pieces from the 1920s and even a few from the 1800s. They also sell jewelry and a nice selection of designer handbags [351 W Broadway].

Taking the Pulse of the Fashion World

43 **Opening Ceremony** is a four-story store that includes the work of many emerging designers. Each year, a different country is showcased here through its creators, in a concept that was inspired by the Olympic Games. Items are expensive, but they provide the visitor with a glimpse of the planet's new trends. I consider this place to be an art gallery rather than a shop [35 Howard St]. You'll also find another location of theirs in the ACE Hotel [20 W 29th St].

Unparalleled Meals on the Go

44

Souen restaurant is my neighborhood canteen. I stopped keeping track of the number of celebrities I've met in this macrobiotic Japanese restaurant; Lou Reed was a regular. I recommend the **Macro Plate** [210 6th Ave]. For a healthy lunch, I stop in at **Chobani**. They serve savory and sweet Greek yogurt-based creations, as well as sandwiches on simit bread, the Turkish version of a bagel [210 6th Ave]. At **Hampton Chutney**, you can taste enormous, paper-thin rice crepes topped with various kinds of chutney. Wash it down with watermelon juice, orange blossom water lemonade and cardamom coffee [143 Grand St].

The best burger in SoHo can be found at **Black Tap**, a small counter with 18 seats where they serve a wide variety of hamburgers and beer on tap [529 Broome St].

Two Hands (A) is a cafe with a clean and simple design where you can order sandwiches, avocado toast, salads, croissants and a large selection of freshly pressed juices. This spot also doubles as an art gallery [164 Mott St].

Fine Dining

45

For market cuisine, I go to **Estela**. Chef Ignacio Mattos apprenticed at California's Panisse, owned by the high priestess of the Slow Food movement, Alice Waters. Try his *burrata* with *salsa verde* dish [47 E Houston St]. **Lure Fishbar** is a basement seafood restaurant located across the street from the **Mercer Hotel**. It feels like being inside a millionaire's yacht [142 Mercer St].

Navy (A), a bistro with barely 50 seats, has a more casual vibe. The maritime-themed eatery specializes in seafood and vegetable dishes. This haunt is just as interesting for brunch. A must-try: the poached eggs with vegetables and grains [137 Sullivan St].

Another good brunch option is **Hundred Acres** for its market dishes and rustic decor [38 Macdougal St].

At **The Dutch** bistro, I like to take a seat at the bar in front of the window, order a cheese plate and a good glass of wine, and take in the SoHo atmosphere [131 Sullivan St].

You would be hard-pressed to find a better ambiance than at the **Charlie Bird** restaurant with hip hop playing and photos of boom boxes on the walls. The menu is Italian-inspired, but is actually very New York: you'll find a bit of everything. Try the chitarra nero (black spaghetti with crab). Its young chef, Ryan Hardy, is one of the New York culinary scene's new *enfants terribles* [5 King St].

For an authentic Japanese restaurant, **Omen** (B) is my destination of choice. This establishment existed long before SoHo became a hip neighborhood. During one of my visits, Yoko Ono sat at the next table [113 Thompson St].

45 A

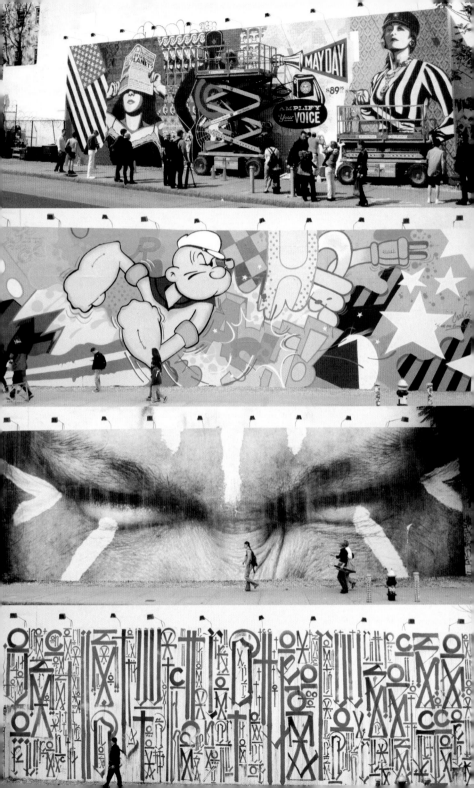

The Artists' Wall

46 The mural located at the corner of **East Houston Street** and **Bowery** is an urban art treasure that's not to be missed. For 25 years, the wall displayed a piece titled *Day-Glo* by Keith Haring, the artist behind the famous primary color silhouettes. Over the last few years, the wall has been repainted regularly—upon invitation from the City of New York—by artists like the Brazilian twins Os Gémeos, Shepard Fairey, photographer JR, Retna and Kenny Scharf. Rather surprising for a city that decided to ban graffiti in 1995.

Toast the Town

47 Caviar, small plates and 150 types of vodka are a good mix at Russian bar **Pravda** [281 Lafayette St]. I recommend **Pegu Club** [77 W Houston St, 2nd floor] for its more refined cocktails that can be enjoyed in a Victorian setting.

The ideal place to kick off the night with a *charcuterie* and cheese plate is certainly the **Compagnie des Vins Surnaturels**, a wine bar with a concept that was developed in Paris. They serve nearly 600 types of wine, including many by the glass [249 Centre St]. If you're looking to have a beer in a legendary New York tavern, go to **The Ear Inn**, which first opened its doors in 1830. People even say that this place—a historic site—is haunted [326 Spring St].

Fanelli Cafe (A), another SoHo institution, has been around since 1922. It's one of the few authentic bars in this neighborhood that became very commercial [94 Prince St].

As for **The Yard**, the SoHo Grand Hotel's small garden decorated with strings of lights, it's the perfect place for a summertime drink [310 W Broadway].

The Temple of Contemporary Art

48 The **New Museum** is the only museum in New York that showcases contemporary art from all over the world. Founded in 1977, they moved into a Bowery tower— designed by a Japanese firm—in 2007. They feature very avant-garde exhibits that are at times too much for my taste. There's an incredible view of the Lower East Side from their rooftop patio, and you'll find a small cafe on the ground floor [235 Bowery]. Across the street, at the **International Center of Photography**, you can check out the works of photographers from around the world. Cornell Capa, brother of war photographer Robert Capa, founded the museum in 1974. Opening in early 2016 [250 Bowery].

The Cheesecake Queen

49 **Eileen's Special Cheesecake** set up shop in 1976. You can try out their mini cakes on the spot, and have of taste of some of the best cheesecake in town [17 Cleveland Pl].

Go Through the Kitchen to Get to the Bar

50 **La Esquina** is a Mexican restaurant with decor that makes the trip worthwhile. From the outside, this place looks like an old 1950s diner. At street level, you'll first see a *taquería* with a sidewalk terrace. Then, after going down a narrow staircase and through a piping-hot kitchen, you'll stumble across a dining room and a dark, rustic bar [114 Kenmare St].

SOHO, NOLITA, LOWER EAST SIDE

51 D

51 B

51 C

51 A

Petrosino Square Restaurants

51 The restaurants around this small park are all good, including **Cafe Select** (A) with an Austrian-inspired menu. During the winter, their cheese fondue and *raclette* are a must [212 Lafayette St]. The owners also run **Rintintin** (B) [14 Spring St], a charming restaurant that serves affordable and delicious Mediterranean-style cuisine. For a healthy brunch, **The Butcher's Daughter** (C) [19 Kenmare St] is one of my favorite destinations, along with **Jack's Wife Freda** (D) [224 Lafayette St]. Simple, delicious and affordable food. For a lobster sandwich, you have to try **Ed's Lobster Bar** [222 Lafayette St]. For the best grilled fish tacos, there's nowhere like **Seamore's**. The restaurant belongs to Michael Chernow, owner of the popular chain The Meatball Shop. All the fish on the menu are from Long Island [390 Broome St].

To see and be seen, Italian restaurant **Sant Ambroeus** [265 Lafayette St] is the eatery of choice for those working in the fashion industry. It's a good option for a coffee, an aperitif or a power lunch in the middle of a shopping spree.

Uncle Boons is the best Thai restaurant in SoHo with decor reminiscent of Bangkok's bazaars [7 Spring St]. Try the crab fried rice.

Osteria Morini [218 Lafayette St] pays tribute to rustic Italian cuisine from the region of Emilia-Romagna. Pasta is handmade, and you should try the charcuterie plate, *gelati* and ravioli stuffed with truffle mascarpone. Divine.

52

Bagels Like in Montreal

52 Noah Bernamoff and Joel Tietolman, two Montrealers who have lived in New York for a few years, opened **Black Seed**—Manhattan's first artisanal bagel bakery—in April 2014. Their bagels are fresh out of the wood-burning oven, and are similar to the ones you'll find on St-Viateur Street and Fairmount Avenue in Montreal. They also make their own cream cheese and smoked salmon [170 Elizabeth St]. Black Seed has a second East Village location in a building previously occupied by an old bakery that opened 110 years ago [176 First Ave].

Multifunction Art Gallery

53 **Clic Bookstore & Gallery** is my favorite gallery in the neighborhood. It's a coffee-table bookshop, an accessories boutique and an exhibition space [255 Centre St].

Mott Street Restaurants

54 **Cafe Gitane** (A) is one of the establishments I patronize most. They serve Moroccan food, and the most coveted tables are outside where you can watch the procession of passersby [242 Mott St]. Across the street is **Saint Patrick's Old Cathedral**, whose construction was completed in 1815. Francis Ford Coppola used the church to film the famous baptism scene in *The Godfather*. Martin Scorsese also filmed the church in *Gangs of New York*. As for pizza, I go to **Emporio** [231 Mott St]. For pasta, **Ballato** [55 E Houston, entrance on Mott St] is my top choice, and I get affordable sushi at **Mottsu** [285 Mott St]. For a pre-dinner drink, I choose **Epistrophy** (B), a spot where many Europeans hang out [200 Mott St].

53

54A

54B

Mulberry Street Restaurants

55 When it comes to restaurants, this is one of the most interesting streets. Israeli chef Einat Admony serves reinvented Mediterranean dishes at **Balaboosta** [214 Mulberry St]. She also owns the delicious falafel counter, **Taïm**, right next door. Even the skeptics will get behind it! [45 Spring St].

Rubirosa (A) is the pizzeria that belongs to Staten Island's pizza guru, Giuseppe Pappalardo. The crust is very thin and crispy [235 Mulberry St].

Torrisi Italian Specialties (B) [250 Mulberry St] is one of the best Italian restaurants in town. The tasting menu with a dozen or so dishes changes seasonally. They make mozzarella in-house and serve it as a warm appetizer. The restaurant next door, **Parm**, belongs to the same owners and has a more affordable menu. Their specialty is the meatball sub, and you should also try the fried calamari [248 Mulberry St].

Tartinery serves toast on Poilâne bread that arrives from Paris on a weekly basis via Fed Ex. An ideal place for lunch or brunch [209 Mulberry St].

Elizabeth Street Restaurants

56

Set in what was once a garage, the Mexican restaurant **Tacombi** (A) serves tacos made in an old Westfalia van [267 Elizabeth St].

The Italian restaurant, **Peasant**, is one of the neighborhood's well-kept secrets. All dishes are cooked in the open-concept kitchen's wood-burning oven, and you'll be served a bowl of fresh ricotta upon arrival. The rabbit and pizza *bianca* are must-tries [194 Elizabeth St]. Step in next door, and you'll find yourself in a Thai restaurant with a setting that feels like a dollhouse. **Lovely Day** also has a bar and a few tables in the basement [196 Elizabeth St], while **Cafe Habana** (B) has been a local institution since 1998. If you don't want to wait for a table, there's a take-out counter right next door. You can sit on a bench outside and order the specialty: grilled corn topped with mayonnaise and *cotija* cheese [17 Prince St].

For brunch, **Egg Shop** (C)—as its name suggests—serves nothing but eggs in all their iterations, whether it's in a quinoa bowl or a fried chicken sandwich. The restaurant closes at 1 a.m. on the weekend [151 Elizabeth St].

56 B

56 C

56 A

The Champion of the Lower East Side

57 **Clayton Patterson** is one of the first New Yorkers I interviewed after I arrived in this city. I was fascinated by the history of the Lower East Side, an area that has changed dramatically in just a few years. Twenty years ago it was the "Far East"—mainly inhabited by junkies, punks and street gangs. The Canadian photographer is the only person who religiously documented the evolution of his adopted neighborhood.

South of **East Houston Street** and east of the **Bowery**, everyone knows "**Clay**." Some have even dubbed him "the mayor of the Lower East Side." He's a rather unexpected mayor, with a biker jacket, baseball cap with embroidered skull, long beard and, of course, a camera bag, which he always carries with him. Here is a man who has literally bled for his neighborhood—and he has the scars to prove it! Clayton has been arrested 13 times by police who took issue with him taking photos. In one instance, they beat him with a nightstick and broke his teeth. "Courtesy of the NYPD," he quipped, showing me his gold teeth.

I met the flamboyant activist in his home at 161 Essex Street, a legendary building in the community. He has lived there since 1983 with Elsa, his partner of 37 years. Together, the couple lives a bohemian lifestyle among their vast archives. The building is packed with boxes containing 2,000 videocassettes, 750,000 photographs, a collection of empty heroin bags and graffiti stickers. The lost soul of the Lower East Side can be found here in this apartment.

Since their arrival in New York in 1979, Elsa and Clayton have documented every heartbeat of the broken neighborhood.

Clayton was 27 when they moved here. He had grown up in a very religious family, and had felt like a stranger in the prairie landscape of his native Alberta.

"It was like the end of the world here," he told me, sitting in the midst of his storage room. "It was so seedy! The night we moved here, a man was shot on the other side of the street," he said, pointing through the window. Yet Clayton is strangely nostalgic for that time. "Crime somehow protected the neighborhood because it kept the rents low. When rents go up, the artistic geniuses are driven out. Today, New York is dead for artists. Go to China!"

Clayton is best known through the images he shot during the 1988 riots in Tompkins Square Park. At the time, the park was nicknamed "Tent City," and it looked like a real refugee camp. When police tried to drive out the homeless, the situation degenerated into chaos. Clayton ended up in jail because he refused to hand over his tapes to the NYPD. As a guest on *The Oprah Winfrey Show*, he shouted "Little Brother is watching Big Brother," brandishing his new weapon—a video camera—for all the world to see. In some ways, it was a precursor to what we saw during Occupy Wall Street, when protesters captured police conduct on video.

Back then, the **Lower East Side** was not a place you wanted to walk around at night, or even during the day. There were serious drug problems, among other things. The neighborhood was a melting pot of gangs (Crips and Bloods), squatters, anarchists, the homeless, prostitutes, bikers and punks.

Clayton entered into all of these worlds at a time when wielding a camera in the

streets took some guts. He and his camera could be found among the skinheads at the Pyramid Club, the hardcore punk crowd at CBGB, backstage at drag clubs, and in an assortment of drug dens—Clayton ventured where no one else would go. Over time, he became the official photographer of the Lower East Side, and so a tradition was born: to be photographed by Clay in front of his graffiti-covered door. People would show up at his door at four in the morning; some even posed with guns. Over the years, Clayton has accumulated thousands of portraits this way. He had no idea, however, that he was also documenting the last breaths of a neighborhood that is now thoroughly gentrified, with its designer shops, luxury condos and hipster bars. At the time, artists like Lou Reed might have paid $38 a month in rent. Today, it would be at least $3,000.

As for Clayton, he no longer recognizes his neighborhood. He now spends most of his time in a small village in Austria, where he has been adopted by an artists' community that reminds him of his old New York.

Clinton Street

59 This is one of the only streets in the neighborhood that's lined with trees. It also has many independent shops, barbers, art galleries, and an establishment said to make the best crepes in town, the **Clinton Street Baking Company** [4 Clinton St].

New Yorkers also line up in front of **Ivan Ramen** for soups made by Ivan Orkin, a Long Island chef who fell in love with Japan. He opened a ramen restaurant that was a huge hit in Tokyo and is now back in New York. Try his bowl of shio ramen or the surprising bowl of four-cheese ramen [25 Clinton St].

Andy Warhol's Glasses

60 **Moscot** is a glasses store that opened its doors in the Lower East Side in 1915. They still sell the same frames that they did in the 1930s or 1950s. This is where you can get your hands on the famous Miltzen frames made popular by Andy Warhol, Harry Truman, John Lennon and Gandhi. That said, the Miltzen cost $6.75 in 1959. Today, they sell for $240 [108 Orchard St].

The Bowery's Graffiti

58 One of the most legendary New York streets is **the Bowery**. Over the last few years, 20 or so artists took it over and painted the metal doors that protect its stores overnight. This is probably one of the city's most colorful streets. Lighting and restaurant equipment stores, old abandoned buildings and a homeless shelter share the artery with new condos, hip shops and art galleries. The Bowery is a perfect example of Lower East Side gentrification.

The Pastrami Sandwich

61 *"I'll have what she's having"* is a line the waiters at Katz's hear often. Founded in 1888, the deli is best known for its pastrami sandwiches, but especially for the famous scene in *When Harry Met Sally* where, sitting across from Billy Crystal, Meg Ryan fakes an orgasm at the table. The movie might have been filmed in 1989, but the decor at Katz's hasn't changed since.

Behind the counter, the neon sign that reads SEND A SALAMI, THAT'S ALL dates back to World War II, a time when **Katz's Delicatessen** shipped goods to American soldiers on the frontlines. At night, you'll rub shoulders with a party crowd facing down mountains of fries. On the weekend, you'll run into tourists and regulars from New Jersey. The restaurant is open all night on Fridays and Saturdays, and closes at three in the morning on Thursdays [205 E Houston St].

People call it "The Bowery," not "Bowery Street." #onlyinNY

61

Mark's Doughnuts

62 **The Doughnut Plant** is a doughnut shop where everything is homemade, right down to the jams. The doughnut flavors here are unusual. For example, you can try ginger, rose petal, pumpkin or coconut doughnuts. My favorite is the peanut butter and jam option. The founder, Mark Isreal, still works there every day. He concocted his first doughnuts in his basement in 1994, following his grandfather's recipe. Martha Stewart once had him on her show and, just before being imprisoned in 2004, ordered a box of his doughnuts. Since then, Isreal has opened locations in Japan and South Korea [379 Grand St].

From Father to Daughter

63 One of my Sunday rituals is to head over to **Russ & Daughters** on East Houston Street, another New York institution. The business has belonged to same family of Polish descendants for four generations. They've been selling smoked fish, caviar and dried fruit since 1914. They're also said to be the first New York business to have written "and daughters" on their sign. The Smithsonian Institution even declared Russ & Daughters to be part of the city's cultural heritage. Order a smoked salmon bagel and eat it while sitting on the bench in front of the store [179 E Houston St]. In the spring of 2014, the family opened the **Russ & Daughters Café**, a restaurant with a wonderfully retro decor where they serve one of the best smoked fish platters in town, as well as many other traditional Jewish dishes [127 Orchard St].

The Candy of My Childhood

64 Founded in 1937, **Economy Candy** is one of the oldest candy stores in New York. They sell sweets from all eras; it's somewhat of a candy museum and the perfect place to feel like a kid again [108 Rivington St].

The Hidden Restaurant

65 To access **Beauty & Essex**, you must first walk through a pawnshop with many guitars hanging on the walls. One of the doors at the back of the store leads to a huge art deco resto-lounge. The menu is made up of small plates to share. Note to the ladies: Pink champagne is free in the bathrooms [146 Essex St].

66 A

The Canteens
of the Lower East Side

66

A charming bistro and one of the many establishments belonging to New York restaurant guru Keith McNally, **Schiller's Liquor Bar** is a good bet [131 Rivington St].

The first French restaurant by two other industry stars—the duo of Italian chefs Rich Torrisi and Mario Carbone—**Dirty French** reinterprets bistro classics. Specialties include the black bouillabaisse, duck à l'orange and roast chicken served with crepes. The restaurant is located in **The Ludlow** boutique hotel, an enjoyable place to grab a drink [180 Ludlow St].

Contra is a restaurant with contemporary cuisine that only serves one five-course, fixed menu that changes seasonally and with the availability of market ingredients. As opposed to other tasting menus in town, the price here is quite reasonable ($55). There are a few à la carte options at the bar [138 Orchard St].

Mission Cantina, the Mexican restaurant of San Francisco's celebrity chef Danny Bowien, serves up excellent tacos and burritos. The decor is festive, the music is loud and the lighting kaleidoscopic [172 Orchard St]. Bowien owns another very sought-after restaurant in the neighborhood, **Mission Chinese Food**, where he concocts Americanized Chinese cuisine in a hip, laid-back atmosphere. He sometimes offers free beer to those waiting in line outside [171 E Broadway].

At **The Meatball Shop** [84 Stanton St], they only sell meatball-based dishes. I love the concept, and you can eat here for under $10. At the **Black Tree** sandwich counter [131 Orchard St], the chef only uses local products, whether it's meat, bread, vegetables or even spices. He makes a daily trip to the Union Square market and gets inspired by the day's products to build his menu. They also serve excellent cocktails.

El Rey (A), a cafe and luncheonette, is no bigger than a shoebox. Chef Gerardo Gonzalez, originally from San Diego, makes wonderful salads, falafel, frittatas and pastries. For a good espresso, I stop in at **Henrie**, graffiti artist André Saraiva's cafe. I love the industrial style of this place that's both a social club and art gallery [110 Forsyth St].

A Mile in the Shoes
of a 19th-Century
Immigrant

67

You can't miss the **Tenement museum** if you want to know how New Yorkers lived in the 19th century. From 1863 to 1935, close to 7,000 people of 20 different nationalities crammed into the building at 97 Orchard Street. In the 1910s, the Lower East Side was one of the most densely populated places on the planet. There was on average 10 people in apartments of barely more than a few square feet. The museum is located in real apartments that haven't changed in over 100 years. It's a bit like time traveling or stepping into a time capsule. The building stands at the civic address 97, but entrance tickets are sold at 103 Orchard Street where you'll also find a souvenir shop.

A Charming and Discreet Alleyway

68

On Rivington Street, between Bowery and Chrystie streets, you'll find **Freeman Alley**, a passageway that leads to one of the best restaurants in town. Freeman's decor includes taxidermy and hunting trophies; it feels like traveling back to the colonial era. The line is often long, but you can take a look at the menswear store at the alley's entrance to pass the time [8 Rivington St].

Clandestine Establishments

69

Kuma Inn (A) is a Thai and Filipino restaurant hidden on the second floor of a building that isn't much to look at. You'll find the door at 113 Ludlow Street, next to an old grocery store. The food is exceptionally good, costs next to nothing, and you can bring your own wine. Good times guaranteed.

The Backroom is a bar hidden behind a fake toy storefront. They serve alcohol in teacups, the style is baroque, and there's a secret room behind a bookcase. It feels like stepping into the Prohibition era. On Monday nights, a jazz band sets the tone [102 Norfolk St].

Fig. 19 is another spot where I enjoy having a cocktail in a speakeasy setting. The bar is located behind an art gallery [131 Chrystie St]. Two blocks north, you'll find the **Experimental Cocktail Club**, a chic lounge that serves 15 or so creative cocktails. On Tuesday nights, musicians play 1950s-era jazz [191 Chrystie St].

There's no sign above the entrance to the bar **Attaboy**. That's intentional. In this very intimate setting where there's no menu, the bartender asks you what your preferences are and whips up a personalized cocktail [134 Eldridge St]. There's no sign in front of **Kitty's Canteen** either. This is a dark and narrow restaurant that serves traditional Jewish food with jazz playing in the background. The decor is eclectic with painted porcelain cat figurines and floral-print wallpaper [9 Stanton St].

Small-Town Charm in the Middle of a City

West Village, Greenwich Village

W 19TH ST

10TH AVE

9TH AVE

W 17TH ST

W 15TH ST

W 13TH ST

GANSEVOORT ST

HORATIO ST

GREENWICH ST

72

JANE ST

BETHUNE ST

75

BANK ST

W 11TH ST

73

PERRY ST

70

HUDSON RIVER

- Sights + photo ops
- Bars + restaurants
- Stores + markets
- Arts + culture
- Activities + walks

New York by Bike

70 In May 2013, the New York landscape was changed by the arrival of 300 **Citi Bike** stations and 6,000 blue bicycles. New Yorkers immediately adopted North America's largest self-serve bike system. It costs $9.95 for a 24-hour pass, and just $25 for a whole week. New York has never been considered a cyclist-friendly city. While the municipality has continually created bike lanes since 2007, the motorist mindset has yet to evolve. Despite new protected lanes, cycling in Manhattan remains a risky endeavor.

Despite Citi Bike's omnipresence, there are still a few independent bike shops, like HUB (Hudson Urban Bicycles). This place is like Ali Baba's cave for lovers of old bikes. You can rent bicycles every day there from 9:00 a.m. to 8:00 p.m. [139 Charles St].

The Bar from Another Era

71 **Chumley's** was a writers' hangout for a long time. Simone de Beauvoir, Scott and Zelda Fitzgerald and Allen Ginsberg were regulars at this bar that opened its doors in 1922. During the Prohibition era, a hidden door allowed customers to flee when police showed up. It was apparently the third New York establishment to receive a liquor license after Prohibition ended. The bar closed in 2007 after the chimney and bar's facade crumbled. It was the type of joint where you felt at home; the owner's dog would sleep by the fire. The owner fought in court for years to get his liquor license back, and as I write these words, he is hoping to re-open [86 Bedford St]. I also recommend that you have a drink at **Highlands**, a Scottish gastropub located a few blocks away from Bedford Street. This place is known for its extensive whiskey selection [150 W 10th St].

The Old Sailor Hotel

72

I stop in at Jane Hotel's **Cafe Gitane** at least once a week [113 Jane St]. The owner loves his many decor items, including the sculpted wooden bar. I recommend the avocado toast on seven-grain bread, vegetable couscous, chicken satay, shepherd's pie (named hachis Parmentier on the menu) and tuna ceviche. Dishes are simple and affordable.

The hotel is an old sailors' residence, and most rooms look like a ship's cabin. The *Titanic*'s survivors once stayed here. With its many taxidermy animals and employees in garb from another era, the lobby reminds me of the universe in Wes Anderson's films. I recommend you have a drink in the old ballroom or at the rooftop bar. The view of the Hudson River is gorgeous.

Venice in New York

73

The **Palazzo Chupi**, a palace worthy of Venice's Grand Canal, clashes with the rest of Manhattan's skyline. In 2007, painter and filmmaker Julian Schnabel decided to have an eight-story pink palace built on the roof of old stables in the West Village [360 W 11th St]. The 4,645-square-meter (50,000-square-foot) palace that looks like a wedding cake houses five condos worth an average of 13 million dollars each, a pool, 180 windows, many Moroccan-style balconies and the largest patios in town. Schnabel himself lives in one of the apartments.

April's Fries

74

Chef April Bloomfield's gastropub, **The Spotted Pig**, is worth the trip if only for their huge plates of fries ($9). These shoelace-thin fries tend to disappear in a matter of seconds. People also go for their Roquefort hamburgers. Jay-Z, Bono and chef Mario Batali are co-owners of the establishment [314 W 11th St].

Don't pronounce
the "w" in "Greenwich."
You have to say "Gren-itch."
#onlyinNY

77

John Lennon's First Apartment

75 When we think of John Lennon and New York, we imagine the Dakota Building where he lived and in front of which he was murdered. But if you wish to see his first New York apartment, head to **105 Bank Street** in the West Village where he and Yoko Ono rented a loft in 1971.

The Street for Epicureans

76 When people ask me where to go for good food in New York, I answer "Any restaurant on Bedford Street in the West Village."
Abbottega is an Italian restaurant [14 Bedford St] where I often eat because I never tire of their black pepper and pecorino spaghetti (the dish is called *Tonnarelli Cacio e Pepe*).

Moustache serves excellent Lebanese cuisine. Dishes cost between $5 and $17, and I love them all [90 Bedford St].

When I go back to the Brazilian restaurant **Casa**, it's to treat myself to their *bobo de camarao*: a shrimp dish with coconut milk and a yucca puree [72 Bedford St].

The Smallest House

77 At **75½ Bedford Street**—right across from the Casa restaurant—stands Manhattan's narrowest house, which is barely 2.9 meters (9½ feet) wide. Built in 1873, it was home to many prominent figures, including anthropologist Margaret Mead, as well as actors Cary Grant and John Barrymore (actress Drew Barrymore's grandfather). The small house was recently sold for 3.25 million dollars. This gives you an idea of real estate prices in New York...

The West Village Mayor

78

Gabriel Stulman got hooked on the restaurant industry while studying at the University of Wisconsin. Back then, he was planning on becoming a professor. Instead, he headed off to New York 13 years ago with the slightly crazy dream of carving out a spot for himself in the restaurant world. It was an ambitious gamble. New York has nearly 20,000 restaurants, and the average lifespan of an establishment is two years. Now, at the head of a mini restaurant empire (**Joseph Leonard, Jeffrey's Grocery, Bar Sardine, Fedora, Perla** and **Montmartre**), you could say that he has succeeded. His establishments are all located in the West Village, so you might run into him on the street. Try the lobster spaghetti at **Jeffrey's Grocery** [172 Waverly Pl], **Bar Sardine**'s hamburger or the green gazpacho at **Fedora** [239 West 4th St].

The Cafe and the Luncheonette

79

Located on one of the prettiest blocks in the West Village, **Cafe Minerva** (A) is a spot where I like to linger over leisurely weekend brunch or a glass of wine. I settle down by one of the windows with my newspapers or laptop and watch the passersby [302 W 4th St]. The proprietors also own **Hamilton's Soda Fountain & Luncheonette** (B) right next-door [51 Bank St]. This place pays tribute to 1940s New York with a large selection of old-fashioned sodas, milkshakes and sundaes. Almost all dishes go for under $12, which is rare in the West Village.

A Huge Hamburger

80 When in the mood for a huge, juicy hamburger, locals go to **Corner Bistro**: an old saloon that stands up to the hip establishments taking over the West Village. It's an experience that each New Yorker should live at least once in their lifetime. Have a seat at the mahogany bar or one of the booths and order a glass of McSorley to go with a burger. At $7.75-$9.75, the eight-ounce burger is a steal for the neighborhood. The best time to go is on a weekday afternoon [331 W 4th St].

One of Keith Haring's Last Pieces

81 Keith Haring, one of the grandfathers of pop art, was an emblematic figure of alternative culture in New York in the 1980s. One of his murals was recently restored and is now accessible to the public. You can find it at the **Lesbian, Gay, Bisexual & Transgender Community Center**. Admission is free. Titled *Once Upon a Time*, the piece was created in 1989 when New York was hit with a huge AIDS epidemic. At the time, the center asked Haring to paint a piece; he chose the men's bathroom on the 2nd floor. The four walls are covered with sexually explicit frescoes. It's therefore preferable to not bring children to see it. Nine months later, Haring died of AIDS at the age of 31 [208 W 13th St]. You can admire another Keith Haring mural at the **Carmine** outdoor public swimming pool. The 50-meter (164-foot) long piece was created in 1987 [1 Clarkson Street].

Brunch, an Italian Feast and Seafood

82 For brunch, I like to grab a table at **Bluestone Lane** (A), a concept that originated in Melbourne, Australia. The chef specializes in healthy and gluten-free food. The buckwheat banana bread topped with fresh ricotta, caramelized pecans, honey and pollen is divine [55 Greenwich Ave]. I also love **Buvette**, chef Jody Williams' *gastrothèque*. Try her *croque-madame* and take a seat in the lovely garden [42 Grove St]. Jody also owns **Via Carota** across the street, a restaurant that dishes out delicious Tuscan cuisine in a rustic setting [51 Grove St].

For Italian cooking, I also go to **Frankies Sputino** [570 Hudson St], **Aria**, an Italian wine bar [117 Perry St] and **L'Artusi** [228 W 10th St], another slightly chicer wine bar. To see and be seen, the Italian restaurant **Sant Ambroeus** (B) is still a top pick for the stars. Have a seat on the patio and be patient [259 W 4th St].

At **Carbone** (C), chefs Mario Carbone and Rich Torrisi reinvent Italian-American classics in decor reminiscent of *The Godfather*. It's the type of place where you could spot Tony Bennett at the next table. Prices are steep, but portions are gargantuan. Try the Caesar salad, veal Parmesan, vodka rigatoni and tiramisu [181 Thompson St].

A few doors down, chefs Carbone and Torrisi also own one of the most decadent establishments in New York, **ZZ's Clam Bar**. The tiny restaurant with 12 seats and a Polynesian decor serves only fish and seafood dishes. Most of the fish arrives straight from Tokyo's Tsukiji Market. Cocktails, concocted by guru Thomas Waugh, are made with top-quality ingredients. There's a doorman here, so you'll need a reservation. I'm warning you, prices are exorbitant, but there's a price to pay for exclusivity in New York [169 Thompson St]. As for pizza, I'm loyal to **Kesté**. Dare to try the Nutella pizza to share for dessert (you won't see it on the menu, you have to ask the waiter). The Naples-born chef also makes gluten-free pizza [271 Bleecker St]. If you're crazy about cheese, **Murray's Cheese Bar**'s menu features all cheese-based dishes and a selection of 50 cheeses à la carte [264 Bleecker St].

When it comes to seafood, I go to **Pearl Oyster Bar** where you can feast on all kinds of oysters. Their lobster roll and sundae are legendary. The space is cramped, so you might have to wait a bit [18 Cornelia St]. If patience is not one of your virtues, check out **Mary's Fish Camp** located six blocks north [64 Charles St].

82A

82B

A Photo Safari

83 The streets of the West Village and Greenwich Village are some of the most beautiful in New York. Here are the ones I like to photograph: **West 10th Street** and **West 11th Street** for their colorful houses [between 5th and 8th Avenue]. Washington Mews, Macdougal Alley, Patchin Place and Grove Court are small, paved, car-free streets hidden behind metal gates like in London. During the 19th century, these alleyways were used to park horse-drawn carriages. Don't miss the delightful garden next to The Church of Saint Luke in the Fields at the corner of Hudson and Grove streets.

Awash in Design and Architecture

84 When I'm in the mood to discover the latest architecture and design trends, I head to the **Center for Architecture**. Established in 2003, the center showcases themed exhibits about New York and its large-scale urban projects. It's a good way to discover the DNA of this incredibly dynamic city [536 LaGuardia Pl]. I usually combine this outing with a visit to the galleries at the reputable **Parsons School of Design**. You can marvel at the work of students, as well as outside artists [66 5th Ave]. Good news: Admission is free at both destinations.

"Houston Street" is not pronounced like the city in Texas, but rather "How-sten." #onlyinNY

85

Little Jamaica

85 If you're seized by the urge for a quick trip to Jamaica without leaving Manhattan, head to **Miss Lily's**, a restaurant that regulars nicknamed the "Jamaican Corner." They put together a Caribbean-inspired menu. I've seen Grace Jones and author Fran Lebowitz there in the past. The waitresses who look like models work in décor that is retro-kitsch . At the juice bar, say hello. At the juice bar, say hello to Melvin, a local star with a contagious smile. The shop section sells jewelry and books about reggae [132 W Houston St].

The Key Master

86 Locksmith Philip Mortillaro owns the smallest commercial building in Manhattan, **Greenwich Locksmiths**: a space that's barely 12 square meters (129 square feet). What makes this spot unique is the work of art that adorns the facade. After two years of meticulous work, Mortillaro recreated the celestial twirls of Van Gogh's *Starry Night* with 20,000 keys that he'd kept over the years. He simply wanted to leave his mark on the neighborhood. "Greenwich Village was the heart of artistic life in New York in the 1960s and 1970s," he says. "Andy Warhol, Keith Haring and Julian Schnabel all lived and created here. Nowadays, rents are too high, and artists have to head out to Brooklyn." Philip told me the anecdote that he once went to Warhol's to install locks on all the windows and doors—after he was the subject of an assassination attempt. [56 7th Ave S].

The Jazz District

87 The best spots to catch a jazz show in the area are **Zinc Bar** [82 W 3rd St], **Smalls Jazz Club** [183 W 10th St], the **Village Vanguard** [178 7th Ave S] and **Blue Note** [131 W 3rd St].

The Oldest Pharmacy in the United States

88 Established in 1838, **C.O. Bigelow Apothecaries** is the oldest American pharmacy that's still fully operational. Inside, you can admire the original wooden cabinets and neo-Gothic gas chandeliers. You'll find many European beauty products and homemade cosmetics that I love. Luminary figures Mark Twain, Thomas Edison and Eleanor Roosevelt were all loyal customers. Now, you might cross paths with actresses like Liv Tyler and Christina Ricci [414 6th Av].

Peanut Butter Heaven

89 At **Peanut Butter & Co.**, they serve mostly peanut butter sandwiches. The menu features 20 different varieties, each one stranger than the last. You'll find a peanut butter sandwich with bacon and pickles, as well as a peanut butter, honey and cinnamon bagel—Jerry Seinfeld's favorite [240 Sullivan St].

An Italian Pilgrimage

90

Bar Pitti should be on the agenda for any visit to New York, especially during the summer because of the terrace. The cuisine hails from northern Italy. Don't be intimidated by the line or rushed waiters, that's part of this place's charm. It's the kind of restaurant where you'll want to hang around for hours on a beautiful sunny day with a mozzarella di bufala appetizer and entrée of boar pappardelle. Be ready for star sightings. You might recognize Jay-Z and Beyoncé or Julianne Moore at the next table. Know that they don't accept credit cards, only cash [268 6th Ave]. If ever the wait is too long, **Cafe Clover** on the other side of the street also has a lovely terrace [10 Downing St].

The Barbers

91

Those who follow me on social media are aware of my obsession with barbershops. However, authentic ones are increasingly rare in New York. My favorites in the West Village and Greenwich Village are **Harry's Corner Shop** (A) [64 Macdougal St], **West Village Tonsorial** [162 7th Ave S], **Fellow Barber** [5 Horatio St] and the classic **Astor Place** that's been in business since 1947. When they opened, there were only five working barbers, now there are 75. Many celebrities, including Alec Baldwin, Matt Damon, LL Cool J and Stephen Colbert patronize this salon, and their photos line the walls. This is a place you absolutely must visit to grasp the multicultural soul of New York. Women are also welcome [2 Astor Pl].

The Hamburger that's Worth its Weight in Gold

92

If you had to treat yourself to only one burger in New York, go for the Black Label at **Minetta Tavern**. As with the best pizza, the best hamburger is a hotly debated subject in New York. However, the one at Minetta Tavern seems to be a unanimous pick. At $28, the Black Label Burger—dry-aged beef, caramelized onions and a brioche bun—is no bargain. This restaurant has been around since the 1930s. F. Scott Fitzgerald and Ernest Hemingway were regulars [113 Macdougal St]. Located on the same street, **J.G. Melon** serves up a much more affordable burger ($12) in a typically New York setting [89 Macdougal St].

The First Cappuccino

93 With the boom of chain coffee shops, it's reassuring to see that places like **Caffe Reggio** keep attracting loyal customers. Opened in 1927, this cafe prides itself in having served the first cappuccino in the United States. Their espresso machine dates back to 1902 and the cafe's walls are adorned with Renaissance period paintings. Setting foot in Caffe Reggio is like taking a trip back in time. It has been used as a setting in many movies, including *The Godfather Part II* [119 Macdougal St].

The Artists' Hotel

94 Built in 1900, right in the heart of Greenwich Village, **Marlton Hotel** hosted—back then, sometimes for months at a time—many artists like writer Jack Kerouac and Beat Generation poets. Kerouac wrote two novels during a stay at this hotel: *The Subterraneans* and *Tristessa*. It has now become a charming boutique hotel. Even if you're not one of the hotel's customers, you can stop in for afternoon tea, coffee at the espresso bar, a wonderful meal at their restaurant, Margaux, or a drink at their marvelous bar. Many cocktails are actually inspired by Kerouac, including the Dharma Bum and Double Rye Manhattan. The hotel, with 107 rooms, is located right by Washington Square Park [5 W 8th St].

From Farm to Table

95 At **Rosemary's** trattoria, everything is made with local ingredients and the produce from the restaurant's rooftop vegetable garden. Try the linguine with pickled lemons, homemade focaccia and olive oil cake [18 Greenwich Ave]. Opened in what used to be a speakeasy (a clandestine bar during the Prohibition era) right by Washington Square Park, the posh **Blue Hill** serves food direct from the bounty of their Hudson Valley farm, where you'll also find a restaurant (see reason No. 300) [75 Washington Pl].

Jiro's Apprentice

96 In the eyes of purists, **Sushi Nakazawa** is *the* sushi counter in New York. Chef Daisuke Nakazawa was apprentice to Jiro Ono in Tokyo, one of the greatest masters in the world. If you can't go to Japan, you can still get a good idea of Jiro Ono's know-how in New York. However, you will need to make a reservation a few weeks in advance, as there are only 10 seats at the bar and 25 at the back of the restaurant. The nine-course meal (21 pieces) costs $120. It's an unforgettable experience; you'll remember each bite of sushi and sip of sake [23 Commerce St].

The Bohemian Artist and Student Neighborhood

NoHo and East Village

- **Sights + photo ops**
- **Bars + restaurants**
- **Stores + markets**
- **Arts + culture**
- **Activities + walks**

EAST
RIVER

E 20TH ST

E 12TH ST 104

E 11TH ST

•103

104 104 103 104 •104   E 10TH ST
104 •   104
E 9TH ST
104   TOMPKINS   •109
                 SQUARE   102 •102
                 PARK
•   AVENUE D
111 AVENUE A

E 6TH ST

FDR DR

EAST VILLAGE   E 5TH ST

E 4TH ST 102

E 3RD ST

AVENUE B

AVENUE C

E 2ND ST   102

E 1ST ST E HOUSTON ST

ORCHARD ST

RIVINGTON ST

NORFOLK ST

ATTORNEY ST

CLINTON ST

RIDGE ST

STANTON ST

PITT ST

COLUMBIA ST

BARUCH ST

DELANCEY ST

BROOME ST

DOWNING
PARK

LEWIS ST

The Mosaic Man

97 Everyone in the East Village knows **Jim Power**. For nearly 30 years, he has been decorating street furniture with recycled materials. He is one of the city's last iconoclasts. "I'm not the last," he says, "I'm the first." It's impossible to walk around the East Village without seeing his work, which decorates everything from planters to street lights to fire hydrants. Each of his pieces pays tribute to the city's heroes and workers, and most can be found in St. Marks Place.

Born in Ireland, Jim arrived in New York in 1959 and grew up in Queens. He fought in Vietnam in the 1970s and worked in construction when he returned from the war. In the 1980s, an injury forced him to give up his work and he found himself in the street, without a home. Today, he lives in transitional city housing in Harlem.

In the 1990s, the city destroyed fifty of his mosaics, which they considered vandalism. Eventually, the authorities decided to allow his works, and now Jim is responsible for restoring each mosaic piece by piece, always accompanied by his faithful dog Jessie Jane. Over the years, he has made nearly 80 mosaics on New York street furniture. Although they are now considered a neighborhood attraction, Jim is concerned that when he dies, no one will take over the job of preserving his work.

While cleaning a lamppost with a sponge in Astor Place, he told me: "I won't be able to do this much longer—my hips won't let me. Working in the streets is a struggle, but I love what I do. New York is my theater. Can you think of a Broadway play that has run for thirty years?"

But still, I wondered, why on Earth did Jim Power choose to decorate the East Village? My answer came from a local walking by: "The East Village chose him!"

For nearly 30 years,
he has been decorating street furniture
with recycled materials.

The Secret Japanese Restaurant

98

Bohemian is a Japanese restaurant hidden behind a butcher shop at 57 Great Jones Street. The building belonged to Andy Warhol and once served as the studio of artist Jean-Michel Basquiat. It was here that he was found dead from a heroin overdose in 1988. The restaurant's phone number isn't listed; you have to get it from someone who has already eaten there. Ask your hotel to make a reservation for you or send an e-mail to ny-info@playearth.jp with "Visit Enquiry" in the subject field. This spot morphs into a lounge with bossa nova and jazz music at around two in the morning. Feel free to join the band after grabbing one of the many musical instruments in the dining room.

Pasta and Cocktails

99

For a drink in NoHo, the **Bowery Hotel** is a classic. The lobby looks like a luxurious Gothic mansion with its Persian carpets, velvet armchairs, marble fireplace and bouquets of peacock feathers. The hotel's Italian restaurant, **Gemma** (A), has a huge terrace that's very popular during the summer [335 Bowery].

Right next door is **Bar Primi**, chef Andrew Carmellini's excellent pasta shop. They prepare over a dozen types of fresh pasta every day. There are large, communal tables for customers who haven't reserved a seat [325 Bowery].

If both these places are full, try **The Standard East Village** hotel's restaurant **Narcissa**, a few blocks north. You can also have a drink on the hotel's terrace or in the illuminated garden [25 Cooper Sq].

The Haunted House

100

The Merchant's House Museum is completely frozen in time, and the only 19th-century family home that's still intact in New York. Nothing has been moved here since 1832. You'll still see the family's original furniture, works of art and personal objects. The house belonged to Seabury Tredwell, a rich merchant who lived with his wife, eight children and four Irish maids. The family lived in this house for nearly 100 years. Gertrude, the youngest Tredwell, stayed there until her death at age 93; she died in her bedroom. Some people say she never truly left the place... Many strange, inexplicable events have since been reported, such as noises and apparitions [29 E 4th St].

Bond and Great Jones Streets

101

These two streets are NoHo's main arteries. With its cobblestones, **Bond Street** has a particular kind of charm. Over the last few years, luxury condos, as well as many restaurants and designer shops, have replaced artists' studios.

The Smile is a bohemian restaurant for a good breakfast or brunch [26 Bond St]. When in the mood for smoked meat, I head to **Mile End** [53 Bond St].

Il Buco Alimentari & Vineria is one of the best Italian restaurants in New York [53 Great Jones St]. **ACME** is popular for its Scandinavian-inspired cuisine. Eat at the bar and finish off the evening in the basement at **ACME Downstairs** [9 Great Jones St].

I also like stopping in at **Filson**: the boutique of the emblematic brand founded in Seattle in 1897. They sell travel bags, camera bags, leather accessories and men's outerwear [40 Great Jones St].

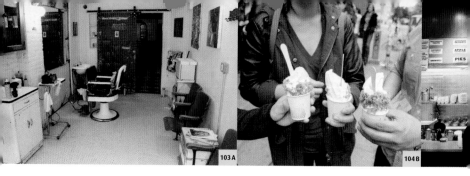

103 A   104 B

The East Village's Community Gardens

102 In the 1970s, an army of green guerillas planted flowers and trees on the East Village's vacant lots that were until then covered with garbage. These oases stood up to real estate development and are now open to the public. There are four on **East 8th Street** between B and D avenues. The most remarkable is the **9th Street Community Garden Park**, which is one of the largest community gardens in New York. The vegetation there is so dense, you can almost get lost in it. I also like the one called **Le Petit Versailles** [247 E 2nd St]. They put on shows during the summer. Madonna fans can go check out her first New York apartment at 232 East 4th Street; she was 20 years old when she moved in.

Beards and Smart Cocktails

103 **The Blind Barber** (A) is both a bar and a barbershop. Visitors enter the watering hole through a hidden door at the back of the salon. They serve delightfully named cocktails like Strawberry Fields and Velvet Underground [339 E 10th St].

For a drink in the area, I also enjoy **Pouring Ribbons** for their impressive list of refined, creative cocktails [225 Ave B, 2nd floor]. At **Booker and Dax**, bartenders use juicers, liquid nitrogen and burners to concoct their cocktails. The bar looks like a mad scientist's lab [207 2nd Ave].

If you want to visit a historic site that's admittedly rather packed, head over to **McSorley's**: New York's oldest tavern, founded in 1854. Women have only been allowed in since 1970, and the decor has remained the same for over a century [15 E 7th St].

102

104 C 104 A 104 D

The Foodie District

104

The East Village is probably the neighborhood with the largest number of restaurants per square foot, and most of them are affordable. For brunch, I really enjoy **Prune**, especially for their fresh ricotta with figs, raspberries, pine nuts and honey [54 E 1st St]. If the lineup seems too long, grab a freshly pressed juice at the stand on the corner of 1st Avenue and 1st Street.

If you're in the mood for pizza, know that **Motorino** [349 E 12th St] makes one of the best in town. The pies at **Gnocco** (A) are pretty good, too [337 E 10th St].

The **Northern Spy Food Co.** is an American bistro with a seasonal menu. The chefs—originally hailing from San Francisco—were inspired considerably by the farm-to-table movement [511 E 12th St].

Maiden Lane—a small restaurant with a Scandinavian design—serves delicious salads, platters of smoked and preserved fish, cheese and charcuterie. Everything is prepared right in front of the guests' eyes [162 Ave B].

I like the pretty terrace at the Brazilian restaurant **Esperanto** [145 Ave C], as well as the one at **Cafe Mogador**, a Mediterranean restaurant where I often go for the couscous and brunch [101 St. Marks Pl].

According to many foodies, the greatest fried chicken sandwich in New York can be had at **Fuku** [163 1st Ave], and the best hamburger is at **Brindle Room**. If you feel like eating some comfort food after a night of partying, it's the place to go.

Chef Jeremy Spector also makes poutine with duck confit [277 E 10th St].

In the healthy restaurant department, I have a soft spot for **Angelica Kitchen** [300 E 12th St], **Quintessence** [263 E 10th St] and the **Liquiteria** juice bar [170 2nd Ave].

The neighborhood's best ice cream can be found at **Odd Fellows** [74 E 4th Street]. For soba noodles, I head to **Sobaya** [229 E 9th St]. And when it comes to ramen, it's all about **Momofuku Noodle Bar** [171 1st Ave] or **Ippudo** [65 4th Ave].

For dumplings, my go-to spot is the brightly decorated **Mimi Cheng's**. Two young sisters opened this restaurant to pay tribute to their mother Mimi's recipes. They make three types of dumplings: chicken and zucchini, pork and bok choy, and vegetable, egg and shiitake. Your meal will barely cost $10 [179 2nd Ave].

For a taste of Christina Tosi's avant-garde desserts like cereal-infused milk, bagel bombs or compost cookies (a treat made with all the ingredients that can be found in a kitchen!), **Momofuku Milk Bar** (B) is the place to go [251 E 13th St].

When I feel like soaking up the East Village's atmosphere, I go to **Veselka** (C), a Ukrainian diner that's open 24/7 [144 2nd Ave]. It's been the neighborhood's eatery since the 1950s. Nightlifers sit down to huge plates of pierogi or bowls of borscht long into the wee hours of the morning.

John's is another East Village institution. The Italian restaurant—with its tiled floor, leather booths and melted candles—doesn't seem to have changed since 1908, the year it opened [302 E 12th St].

The Newsstand Operator

105 **Jerry Delakas** has run the newsstand on Astor Place for more than 25 years. With a sailor's cap, and bent cigarette dangling from his mouth, he looks like a character from a movie. He's always ready to help tourists and even holds on to cellphones for students who can't bring them to class. In 2013, authorities closed the newsstand for 11 months because of issues with his work permit—Jerry, now in his sixties, was born in Greece. New Yorkers would not have it: they signed a petition, plastered his booth with posters demanding his return, and lobbied Mayor Bill de Blasio. In January 2014, the padlock was removed, and Jerry was back.

The Luxury Youth Hostel

106 In my mind, **The Bowery House** is a mix of a youth hostel and boutique hotel. The owners converted the 3rd and 4th floors of an old homeless shelter into a luxurious traveler's sanctuary. This establishment has the advantage of great location. The cabins cost between $67 and $134 a night. During World War II, the then Prince Hotel was reconfigured to temporarily house returning soldiers. So popular were the rooms and the neighborhood, that many never left. [220 Bowery].

The Harley-Davidson Motorcycle Pharmacy

107 The popular beauty products brand **Kiehl's** was launched in the East Village in 1851, and the pharmacy is still in business today. It's truly a museum of antiquated products and a free-sample paradise. Strangely, you can also take a look at a collection of old Harley Davidson motorcycles [109 3rd Ave].

The Timeless Restaurant

108

Indochine has barely changed since the 1980s. Andy Warhol, Madonna and Jean-Michel Basquiat were once regulars here. The restaurant is still just as popular today with models and designers. I remember eating there surrounded by David Bowie, Iman and Marc Jacobs. It is *the* place to go on a Friday night. They serve Franco-Vietnamese-inspired cuisine. Must-try dishes are the Vietnamese bouillabaisse and the Cambodian amok: coconut milk and sole cooked in a banana leaf [430 Lafayette St].

The Best Espresso

109

For a long time, European tourists complained that the only cafes you could find in New York were Starbucks, but now there are independent coffee shops in every neighborhood. My favorites in the East Village are the miniscule counter, **Abraço** [86 E 7th St], **Ninth Street Espresso** [700 E 9th St], **Ost Cafe** for its bohemian vibe [441 E 12th St], and **Everyman Espresso** that acts as an office space for many bloggers. You might catch a glimpse of Ryan Gosling or members of the band The Strokes [136 E 13th St].

Eating in a Christmas Tree

110

Panna II and **Milon** are two Indian restaurants located side by side on 1st Avenue. They've belonged to the same owner since 1990. He's decorated his kitschy temples with enough lights and glowing objects to empty out three hardware stores. Waiters have to weave their way between the wires, and eating here feels like sitting in the middle of a Christmas tree. Thankfully, the food is also very good [93 1st Ave]. In the Gramercy neighborhood, German restaurant **Rolf's** has the same type of decor. It's no surprise that this place is so popular during the holidays [281 3rd Ave].

Open Door, Open Heart

111 Among the characters who have crossed my path since I arrived in this city, **Anthony Pisano** is among those who are at once unique, authentic and totally endearing. I still check in with him from time to time to see how he's doing.

I met Mr. Pisano one evening as I was walking along 7th Street between 1st Avenue and Avenue A. He was sitting in front of the window of what looked like an antique store, a bottle of San Pellegrino at his feet. The door was wide open and the voice of Frank Sinatra poured out onto the sidewalk. With his arms crossed, he watched as people passed by. "Come in, darling," he beckoned. I accepted his invitation and ventured in alone. The dark space, barely larger than a subway car, was packed with items stacked up to the ceiling. When I noticed a bed, kitchen and grand piano, I realized that I was not in a store at all—I was in his apartment. For decades, Anthony has been accumulating musical instruments, old clocks frozen in time, antique jewelry, vintage photographs, and all manner of treasures. His home is a veritable Aladdin's cave, where nothing is for sale.

At first I thought I'd stumbled upon a compulsive hoarder, but I soon realized that—on the contrary—everything at Mr. Pisano's is highly organized, and that he has no attachment to these objects. For him, it's just an excuse to meet people, and he often asks them to take something as a souvenir of their visit.

Mr. Pisano told me he likes to spot couples arguing. He invites them in, then waits for the magic to happen. "It works every time," he said. "They always leave arm in arm."

His door is always open to strangers, which is rather surprising in a city like New York. "This right here is my veranda," he said, referring to his small section of sidewalk. "Nobody has ever stolen from me." "You really trust people?" I asked. "Why wouldn't I?" he responded. Once he even found a young woman asleep on his bed.

"The neighborhood hasn't changed," he explained, "the people have. It's better now. There are no drug addicts and it's a lot safer." He took the bars off his windows twenty years ago.

Born in Sicily, Mr. Pisano landed in New York at the age of 10. He was a musician, and played at the Copacabana in the 1950s. He also served in the merchant navy for 15 years.

When I asked him to tell me about his career, he answered, "I was married for five months, that was my career!" He had six children, all raised by a father who allowed strangers into their home.

Mr. Pisano still rents his apartment at 102 East 7th Street, but the owner has tried to drive him out many times. In the 1980s the rent was about $150 a month.

Now, in this neighborhood, it would be more like $3,000.

If you're in the area, stop by and say hello. He may even send you off with a souvenir, and, more than likely, a "Bye-bye, love" when you return on your way.

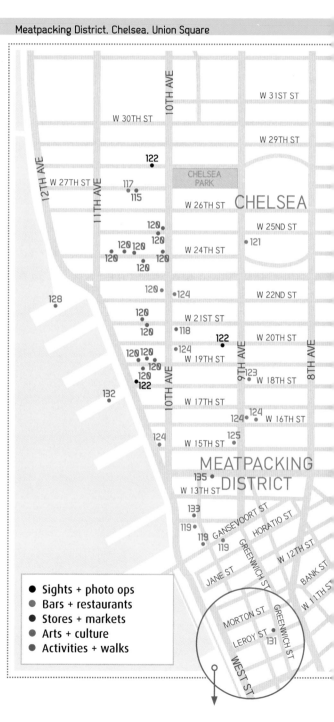

W 31ST ST

10TH AVE

W 30TH ST

W 29TH ST

122

CHELSEA
PARK

W 27TH ST

12TH AVE

11TH AVE

117
115

W 26TH ST

CHELSEA

120

W 25TH ST

120
120

121

120 120
120
120
120

W 24TH ST

120 • 124

W 22ND ST

128

120

120
120

W 21ST ST

118

120 120
120
120
122

124

122

W 20TH ST

8TH AVE

9TH AVE

123
W 18TH ST

132

W 19TH ST

10TH AVE

W 17TH ST

124
125

124 W 16TH ST

124

W 15TH ST

MEATPACKING
135
W 13TH ST

DISTRICT

133

119

119 GANSEVOORT ST

HORATIO ST

119

GREENWICH ST

W 12TH ST

JANE ST

BANK ST

W 11TH ST

● Sights + photo ops
● Bars + restaurants
● Stores + markets
● Arts + culture
● Activities + walks

MORTON ST

GREENWICH ST

LEROY ST

131

WEST ST

The Most Eclectic Square

112 Watching the individuals that hang around **Union Square** is a show in itself. Chess players mix with Occupy Wall Street activists, Hare Krishna followers, artists, break dancers and junkies. People have actually nicknamed the walkway that runs through the park's east side Methadone Alley, since it's usually overrun with drug dealers.

Since 1976, 140 farmers have set up their stalls of organic produce at Union Square on Wednesdays, Fridays and Saturdays. You might cross paths with renowned chefs like Mario Batali (Babbo, Del Posto, Lupa, etc.) running errands.

When I'm in the mood for a picnic at Union Square, I first make a stop at the **Rainbow Falafel** counter, located northwest of the park. Most to-go dishes are vegetarian. I always order the falafel sandwich ($4.50) and a small Turkish coffee ($2.50). The cheerful owner Mohammad Jamal has been making some of the best falafel in New York since 1992 [26 E 17th St].

Take a look at the gigantic work of art that covers a building facade southeast of the park on East 14th Street. **Metronome** is one of the public works of art that's most hated by New Yorkers, who often call it grotesque. To the left of the huge hole from which smoke escapes, a series of 15 glowing numbers scrolls by, some moving slowly, others going at full speed. It's not the countdown clock to the end of the world or a public debt tracker, but rather a very precise 24-hour clock. The first seven numbers tell you what time it is up to a tenth of a second. The other numbers display the time left before the beginning of a new day.

The Cradle of Pop Art

113 **The Factory**, grandfather of Pop Art Andy Warhol's studio, had three iterations in New York, including two at Union Square. Its first location was in Midtown East before moving to the 6th floor of the Decker Building [33 Union Sq W] in 1968. There, Warhol produced his most famous screen-printing and made many films. That's also where he survived a murder attempt. In 1973, he moved his digs a bit further, to 860 Broadway where he worked until 1984. He then moved into his house at 57 East 66th Street where he lived until his death on February 22, 1987.

Wine, Risotto, Tapas and Brownies

114 The surprising restaurant **All'onda** serves Italian fare with Japanese influences. Try their lobster risotto or the *bucatini* pasta dish with smoked urchin and spicy croutons [22 E 13th St]. Spanish restaurant **Boqueria** serves excellent tapas and nice seafood paella [53 W 19th St]. For a drink, **Corkbuzz** is an excellent wine bar and restaurant: the perfect place to try new beverages without breaking the bank [13 E 13th St]. For dessert, **City Bakery** whips up excellent brownies, cookies and hot chocolate [3 W 18th St].

An Evening in the World of *Macbeth*

115

Walk around a hotel with decor from the 1930s with your face hidden behind a mask, witness a murder, experience a bloody ballroom scene, observe passionate acts and discover secret passageways: There's a bit of all that in the **Sleep No More** show. Get ready for a multisensory immersion into the world of Shakespeare's *Macbeth,* created by the Punchdrunk troupe.

A Chelsea warehouse located in an unidentified 27th Street building (an area that was once home to nightclubs like Bungalow 8) was converted into a 1930s hotel, the **McKittrick**. The area measures 10,000 square meters (107,642 square feet), and attention to detail is staggering. Artisans probably worked for four months straight to decorate the five floors. All pieces of furniture are genuine antiques, and the taxidermy animals are from particular collections.

Upon arriving on the scene, a butler will lead you into an art deco bar where 20 or so people will be waiting with a glass of champagne in hand, listening to a jazz orchestra. They'll hand you a white mask reminiscent of *Eyes Wide Shut*. There begins a hallucinatory journey that lasts nearly three hours. Each person moves through the rooms at their own pace, from a child's bedroom to a detective office, candy store, cemetery, ballroom, psychiatric hospital wing or haunted forest.

There are objects to touch, smell and taste in all these spaces. You can open the drawers, rummage through clothing, read letters in search of clues, sleep in Lady Macbeth's bed, and open the closets to discover secret passageways, all within an atmosphere of utmost mystery. Numerous sounds, a movie soundtrack, as well as odors of earth, formaldehyde, dried flowers and blood complete the sensory experience.

Along the way, you'll stumble upon actors silently acting out the scenes of *Macbeth*. Some are true acrobats dancing, as if possessed, amidst the furniture. You can follow them on their course, but they can also latch on to you. A few are completely naked. Some orgy, murder and abortion scenes are so raw that the rooms are open to those age 16 and older only.

That said, don't count on this show for making sense of *Macbeth*. Anyhow, it's impossible to see all the scenes, but one thing is certain*: Sleep No More* will shock your senses and play into voyeuristic tendencies. Tickets cost between $80 and $130 [530 W 27th St].

The Fashion Museum

116

The Fashion Institute of Technology is one of the few museums in the United States that specializes in fashion. The permanent collection includes some 50,000 pieces of clothing and accessories spanning from the 18th century to present day. The students that crowd the school's doors are dressed as if lifted from the pages of avant-garde magazines. Admission is free, but the museum is closed on Sundays, Mondays and holidays [227 W 27th St].

Like a Hitchcock Film

117 Right next to the McKittrick Hotel, you'll find a restaurant called **The Heath** with a menu inspired by traditional British cuisine. If you're looking for a restaurant with a theatrical decor, it's the place to go. You'll feel like you're in a Hitchcockian film noir as you eat in an old train car to the sounds of an improvisational jazz orchestra. Characters can interrupt you at any time to take you into a secret room. The decor—sort of Prohibition-era speakeasy—kind of steals the show from the food, but it's an experience you won't forget. You can finish off the night at the **Gallow Green** bar: their wonderful rooftop garden [542 W 27th St].

Sleeping in a Neo-Gothic Seminary

118 The High Line Park brought about the opening of many restaurants on 10th Avenue, and one of my favorite hotels, the **High Line**. The 60-room boutique hotel is located in an old seminary that was built in 1817. The 1,000-square-meter (10,764-square-foot) refectory is one of the most beautiful spaces in New York. Rooms are furnished with an old-fashioned style, and many have a fireplace. The hotel doesn't have a restaurant, but their cafe, **Intelligentsia Coffee**, is open to the public. There's also a coffee truck—an old 1963 Citroën—in the garden in front of the hotel [180 10th Ave].

119A

The High Line Park

119 This green oasis built on part of an old, defunct railway in southern Manhattan is a point of pride for New Yorkers. Built in the 1930s to transport merchandise, the railroad that overlooks the southwest of the island was abandoned little by little as truck transport increased. The last train—transporting frozen turkeys—ran on the **High Line** in 1980.

For a long time, mayor Rudy Giuliani wanted to demolish this railway. Many celebrities such as Ethan Hawke, Edward Norton, Martha Stewart and designer Diane von Furstenberg supported the West Village's residents in establishing an organization to save it in 1999. Michael Bloomberg's arrival in the mayor's office in 2002 was the project's catalyst. The first section of the park was inaugurated in June 2009, 10 years after the project was first set in motion.

At night, LEDs light up the plants. The park has become so popular that I now prefer going in the evening to avoid the crowd. The High Line is open from 7 a.m. until 11 p.m. every day from June 1 to September 30. You can check opening hours for the rest of the year at this address: thehighline.org/visit.

This linear park has many access points and begins at the corner of Gansevoort and Washington streets. It spans three kilometers (1.9 miles), going all the way to West 34th Street. From up there, you'll glimpse a completely different view of New York City. Between the industrial and residential buildings, you can catch—road permitting—glimpses of the Hudson River and Empire State Building. It's a great way to avoid the traffic, while spying on New Yorkers on their balconies! You might spot an outdoor yoga class, enjoy an ice cream cone, peer into the windows of the great **Standard Hotel**, sit in an amphitheater to

watch the show given by taxis zigzagging along the avenues or take in many artist installations.

The park also caused a real estate boom in the area, stimulating the establishment of many businesses and restaurants, as well as the new **Whitney Museum of American Art** (A), designed by Italian architect Renzo Piano. The 1,205 square meters (12,970 square feet) of outdoor terrace space exhibiting works of art is an addition to the 4,645-square-meter (50,000-square-foot) interior [99 Gansevoort St].

Don't miss **Santina**, the Italian restaurant in a glass cube beneath the High Line (820 Washington St), as well as the neighborhood's last authentic and affordable restaurant located right next door, **Hector's Cafe & Diner** (B). The working class still patronizes the greasy spoon to this day. You can spot the establishment in the TV series

Law & Order [44 Little W 12th St]. A few steps away, you'll find **Gansevoort Market**, a 750-square-meter (8,073 square-foot) food court with many stalls where you can eat lobster sandwiches, tacos, crepes, sushi and macaroons [52 Gansevoort St].

Touring the Galleries

120 **Chelsea** has approximately 200 art galleries on the block between 10th and 11th avenues, and 20th and 27th streets. A piece of advice: It's nice to tour them on Saturdays, and they are also free. However, most galleries are closed on Sundays. Download the free Chelsea Gallery Map app to find the address and current exhibit of each gallery.

Here are my favorite galleries...

For contemporary art and to discover international artists: **Andrea Rosen** [525 W 24th St], **David Zwirner** [519, 525, 533 and 537 W 19th St], **Gagosian** [555 W 24th St and 522 W 21st St], **Mary Boone** [541 W 24th St], **Mike Weiss** [520 W 24th St], **Pace Gallery** [508 W 25th St] and **Gladstone Gallery** [515 W 24th St and 530 W 21st St]. For photography: **Yossi Milo** [245 10th Ave]. To sate your post-tour appetite, I recommend **Juban,** and its art-adorned walls, where you can choose from a wide variety of reasonably priced small Japanese dishes and sakes [207 10th Ave].

A Pizza You Won't Forget

121 I ate the greatest pizza in New York at **Co.,** one of the best-kept secrets in town. The restaurant belongs to Jim Lahey, nicknamed the "master of bread." Try the Popeye, Margherita or Shiitake pizza [230 9th Ave]. The sculptor-turned-baker also owns Sullivan Street Bakery right next door. It's the ideal place for sandwiches. Their Caprese and Pollo Club panini are close to perfection [236 9th Ave].

Greek Renaissance and "Starchitect"

122 Chelsea has the most beautiful modern buildings in New York. The most famous one, the **IAC Building**, looks like an iceberg and was designed by **Frank Gehry** [555 W 18th St]. Next door, you'll find the residential building designed by **Jean Nouvel**. The facade is made up of 1,647 glass panels of different shades of blue [100 11th Ave]. A bit farther north, you can check out the futuristic tower by Iraqi architect **Zaha Hadid**. The building reminds me of the house in *The Jetsons* [520 W 28th St].

If there's a must-see street in this neighborhood, it's **Cushman Row** with its seven neo-classical (or Greek Revival) homes on West 20th Street between 9th and 10th avenues. Built in 1840, these houses are among the oldest in Chelsea [406-418 W 20th St].

A Cocktail in a Bathtub

123 **Bathtub Gin** is a bar hidden behind the **Stone Street Coffee Company** counter on 9th Avenue. There's a copper bathtub in the middle of the bar if you care to take a seat. It's a wink to the Prohibition era when people made alcohol in bathtubs. The list features many gin-based cocktails and a few tasty dishes. I prefer going on weeknights in order to avoid the crowd. They usually play hip-hop [132 9th Ave].

122

The Best Restaurants

124 The best tapas in New York can be had at **Toro**, a 120-seat restaurant located in an old factory. The menu features 59 options of modern and traditional tapas, as well as a large selection of gin and tonics. The service is impeccable [85 10th Ave].

In the summertime, I like eating on the large terrace at Mario Batali's Italian restaurant **La Sirena**. It's one of the rare spots in New York where you can get a table without a wait even if you don't have a reservation. The restaurant is located in the **Maritime Hotel**. I also recommend that you take a look at their retro-nautical lobby [363 W 16th St].

In the basement of the **Dream Hotel** next door, you'll find **Bodega Negra**, an excellent Mexican restaurant with a dark, eclectic decor, and a menu inspired by Yucatán cuisine. Save some room for their famous dessert, the Don Huevo: a chocolate cake hidden beneath a white chocolate globe that they melt by pouring hot caramel over top [355 W 16th St].

Another top restaurant with a large terrace is **Cookshop**, located close to High Line Park. The seasonal menu is made up of local ingredients. They boast a nice selection of both alcoholic and virgin cocktails [156 10th Ave].

Empire Diner (A) is a restaurant emblematic of New York in the 1940s. It shows up in many movies, including Woody Allen's *Manhattan* and *Home Alone*. Must-tries: the smoked salmon and burrata plate, the French onion soup and the Patty Melt [210 10th Ave].

The Food Lovers' Hangout

125 **Chelsea Market** is a big food court located in the old Nabisco cookie factory, and it's New York's version of San Francisco's famous Ferry Building Marketplace. Chelsea Market occupies a whole city block. You can enter at the corner of 9th Avenue and 15th Street, and exit at 10th Avenue. My favorite stalls are **The Lobster Place** for seafood, **Beyond Sushi** for vegan sushi made with black rice, **Lolo Organics** for healthy smoothies, **Amy's Bread** for sandwiches, **Friedman's** for brunch and the coffee counter, **Ninth Street Espresso**. Don't forget to throw a penny into the fountain, located in the center of the market; it's said to bring good luck.

The Urban Jungle

126 The flower district is no longer what it was in the 20th century, but you'll still find a few sellers on **28th Street** between 6th and 7th avenues. The sidewalks are taken over by plants and exotic trees. I love walking around this area and going into each shop; it feels like being in a tropical country. Most businesses have barely changed since the 1890s. If you pay close attention, you could spot signs from that era.

You won't get separate checks in New York restaurants. A single bill arrives on the table, and diners usually split it into equal parts even if one person only ate a simple salad, while the others stuffed themselves with caviar. I've been had many times...
#onlyinNY

124A 125

The Vintage Mecca

127

New York Vintage acts as a costume shop for many films and television shows (*The Great Gatsby*, *Boardwalk Empire* and *Sex and the City*). Located on the antique dealers' street and visited by stylists to the stars, this shop is a small fashion museum. Owner Shannon Hoey has gathered one of the largest collections of vintage designer clothing in New York. You'll find a wide selection of pieces from the 1920s. It's open to the public [117 W 25th St].

If instead you're looking for a costume, a trip to **Halloween Adventure** should be on your agenda. They're open all year long, and it's one of the largest costume stores in New York [808 Broadway].

Sake and Sushi Tasting on a Sailboat

128

For about $100, you can set sail on a large schooner for an on-deck tasting of restaurant **Morimoto**'s sushi, paired with many types of sake. It's an unforgettable experience. The Morimoto cruise leaves from Chelsea Pier [Classic Harbor Line, Pier 62, at 22nd Street], from April until the end of November. The sailboat goes down the Hudson—all the way to the Statue of Liberty—at sunset (sail-nyc.com).

126 128

New York's Favorite Morning Man

129 Pat Kiernan is "Mr. Congeniality." His playful, boyish smile peeks out from behind his serious anchorman's suit. The Canadian-born TV personality, now 47 (in 2016), has been appearing as the morning news anchor of NY1 since 1997. He is part of the morning routine for more than one million New Yorkers.

Mr. Kiernan doesn't assume the forced cheerfulness that seems mandatory on major network morning shows; rather, his appeal stems from his well-placed, subtle sarcasm. "I don't pretend to be happy all the time. New Yorkers don't like being bombarded with jokes; they prefer a subtle, more refined humor," explained the host. He also has a fondness for pop culture: "I have never been one of those journalists with a capital 'J' who refuses to read *People* magazine."

It's no wonder that he's become the darling of popular blogs like Gothamist, and especially Gawker, which has called him "unironically beloved," "Bieber for adults" and "the greatest newsman in New York." Every July 1, he becomes the "token Canadian" on blogs featuring America's northern neighbors.

What secured the success of his morning show was a simple eight-minute segment called *In the Papers*. In it, he summarizes the news items he thinks are worthwhile—and there is always something for everyone. In 2009, the segment also took the form of a popular website, patspapers.com.

The day I met the Pat Kiernan, he had been up since 2:30 that morning. By 4 a.m. he was at NY1, in the Chelsea Market building, and from 5 to 10 a.m. he was on the air. This has been his morning routine since 1997.

"I've tried everything, and the method that works best for me is to take a two-hour nap in the afternoon and go to bed at eleven at night. I don't need much sleep." He seems to be a member of the "sleepless elite." And here's a rather shocking detail for a morning man: Pat Kiernan does not drink coffee.

"Even after all these years, it isn't natural to wake up at 2:30 in the morning, but I still believe that it's the best time slot to do my job. We manage to build really personal relationships with our audience." Jerry Seinfeld is among his faithful listeners.

Born in Calgary in 1968, Kiernan studied business at the University of Alberta in Edmonton, where he worked in radio and television for a few years before moving to New York in 1996 to host the Fortune Business Record on NY1, Time Warner's all-news channel. The following year, he moved to the morning show. Over the years, he has been courted by other major US and Canadian networks, but has remained dedicated to NY1. Pat Kiernan is one of the few Canadians who are prominent in the New York media. Now that Peter Jennings and John Roberts have left, only Ali Velshi, from Al Jazeera America, and Pat remain.

September 11, 2001 is still the defining moment in his career. "That morning I was far from suspecting that the next commercial break wouldn't happen for another three weeks." That tragic day he was on the air for 15 hours straight.

The Last Hippie Stronghold

130 Leonard Cohen sang "I remember you well in the Chelsea Hotel" in the 1970s as an homage to the famous building where he wrote some of his greatest songs. For 130 years, the 23rd Street hotel with Victorian Gothic architecture was a gathering place for poets, painters and punks. Everyone passed through this place, including Bob Dylan, Jimi Hendrix, Janis Joplin, Jim Morrison, Édith Piaf, Joni Mitchell, Jean-Paul Sartre, Arthur Miller, Stanley Kubrick, The Ramones and, of course, Leonard Cohen. Rufus Wainwright once lived in the apartment at the hotel sign's letter *E* level. His room was apparently constantly flooded with red light, like in the famous *Seinfeld* episode.

The Chelsea was built between 1883 and 1885, and was the highest apartment building in town at the time. In 1905, it was partially converted into a hotel.

Its thick walls are probably what attracted artists and musicians. The top floor actually only had artist studios due to the ceiling height. However, Stanley Bard also had something to do with that. Director of the hotel as of 1955, he was known for hosting painters for free in exchange for their work. This is how he built the large collection of works of art that decorated the walls of the hotel and lobby.

That said, the Chelsea's real hidden treasure can be found at its top. Some tenants lived in attics converted into penthouses that were only accessible from the roof. Each had a garden with a breathtaking view of the city: a small flower-and-wrought-iron paradise.

130

The Chelsea Hotel housed an entire eccentric world: dogs everywhere, residents with round glasses who looked like Bob Dylan, multi-colored grannies on electric scooters in the hallways and employees as old as the furniture.

During 30 years on the job, receptionist Jerry Weinstein has seen just about everything: tenants keeping monkeys and snakes, suicide in the stairwell, and Nancy Spungen's vile murder in 1978, possibly at the hands of her boyfriend Sid Vicious of the Sex Pistols. The young woman was found stabbed in the bathroom of room No. 100. He died of a heroin overdose four months later, before his trial.

Over the last few years, the Chelsea has undergone major renovations that have transformed it into a boutique hotel. The re-opening is planned for 2017. Some tenacious residents were able to hold on to their apartment despite the work. They make up what is referred to as New York's last bohemian bubble.

Art and Fashion Replace...Meat

131 **The Meatpacking District** is an area that was once home to slaughterhouses, meat packers, drug dealers and prostitutes. In the 1990s, it was best not to venture too far into it. Nowadays, fashion dominates. Boutiques by designers like **Diane von Furstenberg**, **Alexander McQueen** and **Stella McCartney** have replaced old warehouses.

On Washington Street, an art gallery took over the premises from **Pat LaFrieda**, a meat wholesaler that occupied the spot for 75 years. It's one of the strangest things I've ever seen in New York. The space has stayed the same, but now hosts avant-garde exhibits. A "meat juice" smell still emanates from the walls. It's barely tolerable "but it's a part of the experience," explains the director of the **Gavin Brown's Enterprise** gallery [620 Greenwich St].

133

The Soviet-Looking Boutique Hotel

133 Rooms at the **Standard**, a popular hotel, are insanely expensive, but that's not to say that you can't take advantage of the premises. On the ground floor, you'll find the **Standard Grill** restaurant and **Biergarten**, a sought-after spot during the summer. The popular nightclub **Boom Boom Boom** (A) is on the 18th floor. When they opened, some deemed this place the "new Studio 54," Manhattan's famous 1980s disco.

Up there, the decor is reminiscent of a James Bond film with its beige leather booths, white grand piano, egg-shaped golden fireplaces and waitresses dressed like flight attendants. However, it's difficult to get your foot in the door. The easiest way to do so is to reserve a table between 6 p.m. and 9 p.m. when the bar is open to all. There's also an outdoor disco with a 360-degree view of Manhattan, **Le Bain** (B), on the same floor. This spot is very popular for happy hour during the summer. In winter, they have a street-level skating rink on The Standard Plaza [848 Washington St].

The hotel even offers a summertime seaplane transportation service that can get you to the Hamptons in 45 minutes. It's obviously not cheap (stndair.com).

Hitting Golf Balls in Manhattan

132 Built on an old pier by the Hudson River (between 17th and 23rd streets), **Chelsea Piers** is the largest sports facility in New York. That's where the *Titanic* was supposed to dock in April 1912. In 1995, Chelsea Piers' huge depots were converted into sports installations. Now, you can go there to skate, play soccer, tennis and basketball, do yoga, and take a dance or sailing class. There's also a kid's gym, and it's a wonderful place to hit golf balls. The individual pens are spread out over four floors facing the river. The Golf Club is heated and open year-round, until midnight every day from March to October. Off-season, it closes at 11 p.m. I recommend going at sunset (Pier 59–18th St).

132

133 A

133 B

The Nightlife Guru

134

Twenty years of New York nightlife leaves its mark. "In 1992, I was shot at in a night club. The bullet skimmed my forehead, and I still have a scar," Jeffrey Jah recounts, pointing to the old wound. He tells the story as if it had been a simple trip to the dentist.

Jeffrey Jah was born in Vancouver and spent his childhood in Toronto. At the age of 14, he was going out to alternative music clubs and organizing parties throughout the city. At 16, he dropped out of school and moved to New York, where he discovered the clubs of the time, like Paradise Garage, Milk Bar, Area, and The World. "When I saw those clubs, the whole scene just blew me away." He still remembers the day he moved for good: August 15, 1989. "When I moved out, the telephone companies were on strike so I couldn't call my parents for like three months. They were freaking out!" Then he started organizing parties at three nightclubs: Tunnel, USA and Danceteria. "I brought in bands like the Smashing Pumpkins and Pearl Jam for almost nothing. People did a crazy amount of drugs back then. New York in the 1990s was like the Wild West. There was a crack and heroin epidemic—particularly in the Lower East Side." Today, New York is one of the safest cities in the United States. A little too safe for Jeffrey's taste. The gentrification of certain neighborhoods has made life difficult for club owners. He cites the example of the famous Meatpacking District.

"We opened the Lotus Club in 1999, when the Meatpacking District was full of drag queens, prostitutes, and drug dealers. Gradually, the neighborhood became trendier: the Pastis bistro and designer boutiques opened up. The streets became cleaner and safer. Then there was the housing boom. And now, tenants in luxury condos complain about the noise. You want to live in a trendy neighborhood? Well, there's a price to pay. We've forgotten that New York is the city that never sleeps."

New Yorkers tend to go out on weeknights especially. "People who live here work hard and play hard. Life is really stressful, and most people are single so they're not ready to go to bed right after work," Jah explains. They also want to avoid mingling with the suburbanite crowd who commute to Manhattan on weekends, and are referred to as "bridge and tunnel people."

In New York, where the average lifespan of a restaurant or nightclub is two years, Jeffrey Jah seems to have found the recipe for longevity. Some of his clubs, such as Lotus, have been going strong for 10 years, and he now owns The Lambs Club and Beautique, two restaurant/ lounges in Midtown.

The Other 9/11 Museum

135 **Gary Marlon Suson** was the only photographer who gained access to Ground Zero to document the search for firefighters in the months that followed the September 11, 2001 attacks. He kept nearly 3,000 photos and objects that he now displays to the public in what is called New York's "smallest big museum."

The **Ground Zero Museum Workshop** in the Meatpacking District might only measure 100 square meters (1,076 square feet), you'll leave there shaken. What was once Suson's studio is now packed with relics that speak to the horror, each object the subject of a story told by the photographer in an audio guide.

For example, you can see the clock found in the train station beneath the World Trade Center with the hands stopped at 10:02:14, the moment at which the South Tower collapsed. You can also see a piece of the plane's fuselage that was embedded into the North Tower, and a vintage beer can found in the rubble (workers had hidden many cans of Rheingold between the beams during the tower's construction at the end of the 1960s or beginning of the 1970s). There are also rare glass pieces of the WTC. These are rare since 99 percent of the 43,600 windows were reduced to dust.

In 2001, Gary was no longer just a fashion photographer from Chicago, and occasional actor and scriptwriter. In the days following the attacks, he published photos of the city in mourning on the septembereleven.net website. The New York firefighters' union noticed his photos and decided to entrust him with an exceptional responsibility: accessing Ground Zero for seven months to document the search for the 343 missing firefighters. There were, however a few conditions: he would not be paid, he would not be able to publish his photos until the end of the search, and profits would go to charities supporting the victims' families.

Gary had no idea about what lay ahead. This man who walked through a parallel universe for seven months, spending 16 to 19 hours a day in the belly of the beast surrounded by dead people, is still psychologically scarred. He cried alone at night when he got home. "I had no one to talk to, no one who understood what was going on there." From 2002 to 2005, he suffered from severe depression. "It was too heavy to bear, and I wanted to leave on five different occasions. I wasn't prepared for that, I'm not a first responder."

That said, there were moments that pushed him to persevere. For example, when he found a page of the bible amid the rubble, 80 feet below ground. It was a passage about the Tower of Babel from Genesis. This sentence was highlighted in yellow: "And the Lord said: *If as one people speaking the same language...*" "I interpreted it as a sign," says Gary.

It was during a visit to Holland in 2004, while in the house of Anne Frank, that he got the idea to do the same thing in New York. "The tears that are shed in my museum are a part of the healing process. If we can't internalize the catastrophe, we can't heal," he believes.

The price of admission is $25, and the proceeds go to six different charity organizations in charge of providing relief to the firefighters' families GroundZeroMuseumWorkshop.com [420 W 14th St, 2nd floor].

Posh New York and Emblematic Buildings

Flatiron District,
Gramercy Park

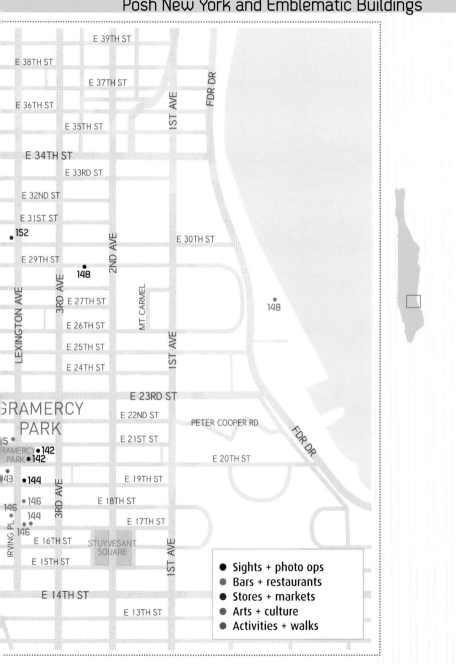

E 39TH ST
E 38TH ST
E 37TH ST
E 36TH ST
E 35TH ST
E 34TH ST
E 33RD ST
E 32ND ST
E 31ST ST
•152
E 30TH ST
E 29TH ST
•148
E 27TH ST
E 26TH ST
E 25TH ST
E 24TH ST
E 23RD ST
E 22ND ST
PETER COOPER RD
E 21ST ST
E 20TH ST
E 19TH ST
E 18TH ST
E 17TH ST
E 16TH ST
E 15TH ST
E 14TH ST
E 13TH ST

1ST AVE
FDR DR
2ND AVE
3RD AVE
LEXINGTON AVE
MT CARMEL
IRVING PL

148

GRAMERCY PARK
5•
RAMERCY •142
PARK •142
43
•144
•146
146
144
146

STUYVESANT SQUARE

● Sights + photo ops
● Bars + restaurants
● Stores + markets
● Arts + culture
● Activities + walks

Most New Yorkers don't own a car, so the sidewalks become their highways. Pedestrian flow must be fast and constant. Those who want to stop and look upward need to step off to the side. New Yorkers never look up. #onlyinNY

A Quick Trip to Italy

136 **Eataly** is a 4,000-square-meter (43,060-square-foot) indoor market located in a historic Flatiron District building. This new temple of the Slow Food movement—originally from Turin—is entirely dedicated to Italian gastronomy. You can try out two cafes, a *gelateria*, bakery, seven restaurants—including a pizzeria, and all the Italian products you ever dreamed of. There's a resto-bar on the rooftop (Birreria), the perfect place to enjoy a beer at the end of the day or to eat under the stars [200 5th Ave].

A bit farther south on Broadway, you'll find **Obicà**, a mozzarella bar where I ate the best mozzarella di bufala campana in all of New York. The precious cheese is delivered twice a week from a farm in Campania, Italy. All dishes are prepared with top-quality ingredients, right before the patrons' eyes like at a sushi bar [928 Broadway].

An Unforgettable Meal in a Carpet Store

137 **ABC Kitchen** is located in **ABC Carpet & Home**, a very chic furniture store and family business founded in 1897. It's my favorite restaurant in New York. If you can treat yourself to only one good meal in town, this is where you need to go. I especially like the decor with its wooden beams, white brick walls, numerous chandeliers and mismatched, flower-patterned dishware. Chef Jean-Georges Vongerichten uses only organic ingredients from local farms. Try the crab spread with lemon aioli, the ricotta appetizer, roasted carrot and avocado salad, and spinach and goat cheese pizza [35 E 18th St].

Madison Square Park

138 **Madison Square Park** is located on East 23rd Street between Madison and 5th Avenue. You can see sculptures and interactive installations there all year-round. During the summer, head over for a picnic and a great view of the Empire State Building. I go there especially for the popular **Shake Shack** (at the southeast corner of the park), the most sought-after snack bar in New York for the last 10 years. Order a burger with a frozen custard. You can even check the size of the line on their website (shakeshack.com) before heading over. A camera—the Shack Cam—broadcasts live images of the stand.

COCTELES | MEZCAL | CERVEZA

139

A Pre-Shopping Retro Lunch

141 "Raising New York's cholesterol since 1929," is **Eisenberg's Sandwich Shop**'s ironic slogan. Right in the heart of the Flatiron District, the narrow luncheonette specializes in pastrami sandwiches, tuna melts and American breakfasts. Thanks to the friendly owner Victor, this establishment hasn't lost its soul or authenticity. I stop in sometimes to sit at the retro counter for a cup of coffee [174 5th Ave]. Then, I head down 5th Avenue toward Washington Square Park to window-shop. **Fifth Avenue** south of 23rd Street has some gorgeous beaux arts buildings. It's also a good shopping destination, far less busy than Midtown.

The Quick Trip to Mexico

139 If you're more in the mood for Mexican food, **Cafe El Presidente** is right next to Eataly. This taqueria, juice bar and grocery store is reminiscent of a Mexican market. Tortillas are made on the premises, and the menu features 12 kinds of tacos, along with various cocktails made with freshly pressed juice [30 W 24th].

Ping-Pong and Cocktails

140 **SPiN** is a popular ping-pong club founded by actress Susan Sarandon. You can play ping-pong while sipping on a cocktail or watching a professional match. The establishment has 17 tables, a bar, restaurant and VIP room. SPiN is open to all during the daytime, but only to people who are 21 and older after 9 p.m. [48 E 23rd St].

The Last Private Park

142 Do you want to catch a glimpse of the lifestyle of New York's elite? I suggest you take a stroll around **Gramercy Park**, Manhattan's last private park. Opened in 1831 and protected by a fence since 1833, it's inspired by London's squares. You need a key to access it, and only residents who live around the park have one. However, guests of the **Gramercy Hotel** next door can also access the square simply by putting in a request with the concierge. If you're not staying at that hotel, you can still take a look at the park through the gate [E 20th St, east of Park Ave]. The houses that surround it are among the most coveted in town. The white building at 36 Gramercy Park East is a neo-Gothic terra cotta masterpiece.

If you see a star, pretend you don't notice. New Yorkers never fix their eyes on them, they are too cool-headed. Unlike in Los Angeles, the stars enjoy relative anonymity in the streets of New York. #onlyinNY

143

The Block Beautiful

144 This is what the section of **East 19th Street** east of Irving Place is nicknamed. With its eclectic mix of colorful houses, this stretch of street is one of the city's most photogenic. I particularly like the architecture around Stuyvesant Square a bit farther east still. There's a charming bed & breakfast on Irving Place in a house that was built in 1834. **The Inn** is one of the most romantic hotels in New York, and each room has its own fireplace [56 Irving Pl].

The Art Lovers' Club

143 On the south side of the park is where you'll find **The National Arts Club**, a private club for artists and patrons founded by author and poet Charles De Kay in 1898. In New York, being a member of a private club brings social status. Many stars, such as Martin Scorsese, Robert Redford and Uma Thurman, are members. Woody Allen also shot *Manhattan Murder Mystery* here.

I once visited the club, pretending that I wanted to sign up. I discovered a place where time had remained frozen in a distant past. The five-story house is classified as a historical monument, and much of its furniture dates back to 1840. There's artwork everywhere. The club's four art galleries are open to the public free of charge from 10 a.m. to 5 p.m., Monday to Friday. You can also take drawing classes on weeknights for about $15 [15 Gramercy Park S].

The Rooftop Garden

145 **The Gramercy Park Hotel** is one of the most beautiful hotels in Manhattan. Its covered garden on the top floor is a real gem. You can have breakfast there surrounded by exotic plants or enjoy an evening drink as you look out at the amazing Chrysler Building. **Maialino**, the hotel's ground-floor restaurant, is one of the best Italian eateries in town, whether you're in for brunch or dinner. The service is very attentive [2 Lexington Ave].

145

Tapas, Cocktails and Taverns

146

Casa Mono is an excellent Spanish restaurant that serves Catalan cuisine and many specialties from the Iberian Peninsula. Try the duck egg with black truffle and the steak with onion marmalade. The restaurant's annex, **Bar Jamon**, serves tapas, Iberian ham and many cheeses. The packed counter is reminiscent of Barcelona tapas bars [52 Irving Pl].

Since 1994, **Gramercy Tavern**—one of restaurateur duo Danny Meyer and Tom Colicchio's great successes—has been among New York's top-rated restaurants. They cook seasonal, American cuisine made with local ingredients and a wide variety of cheeses. The restaurant has two rooms, **The Dining Room**, which only serves a tasting menu, and **The Tavern**, where dishes are of the same quality, but more reasonably priced [42 E 20th St].

New York's oldest restaurant, **Pete's Tavern** (A), opened its doors in 1864, as you can see from the photos on the walls. To feast on a good steak in an authentic setting, this is the place to go [129 E 18th St].

Stepping into the cocktail parlor **Dear Irving** feels like traveling back in time. The concept was inspired by Woody Allen's film *Midnight in Paris*. The bar is divided into four rooms that evoke distinct time periods: 1961, 1923, 1857 and 1772. You can therefore move from John F. Kennedy's world into Jay Gatsby's, Emma Bovary's, and that of the French aristocracy [55 Irving Pl].

The Blushing Museum

147 In the city that never sleeps, it should come as no surprise to find a museum dedicated to sex. The **Museum of Sex** (MoSEX) showcases temporary and permanent exhibits, including one on the sex lives of animals, as well as an impressive collection of sex toys from throughout the ages. The museum is also home to a resto-bar, **Play**, where they serve aphrodisiac cocktails. The Pareidolia is supposed to taste like a freshly shaven man who just smoked a cigarette. You don't drink it in a glass; instead, you lick the viscous liquid from a plate that looks like skin... [1 E 27th St].

Eating Alfresco in Kips Bay

148 **Riverpark** is one of the few New York restaurants where you can eat outside, by the water. The big terrace and outdoor bar make for a spectacular view of the East River and its many bridges. This establishment, one of the few attractions in a rarely visited neighborhood, belongs to New York restaurateur Tom Colicchio, cofounder of the reputed restaurant Gramercy Tavern. The menu is seasonal, and ingredients are from local farms. A must-try for brunch: the breakfast sandwich with scrambled eggs, arugula, pork belly and cheddar [450 E 29th St].

When walking along 29th Street, don't miss the architectural complex made up of a white house and shed registered with the National Monuments Centre. It's one of New York's last wooden houses. Historians don't agree about its construction date, but some claim it to be 1790. Sadly, you can't visit this private residence [203 E 29th St].

Seoul, Steps Away from the Empire State Building

149 In this tiny Manhattan neighborhood between Broadway and 5th Avenue, with 32nd Street as its center point, South Korean culture dominates. Just like in Seoul, **Koreatown**'s businesses are stacked one on top of the other, and you can find karaoke clubs and barbecue restaurants open late at night. Not-to-be-missed gastropub **Hanjan** concocts a cuisine that's both traditional and modern. Take a seat at the large communal table and order a plate of chicken wings (their specialty), the spicy cod bowl (a seasonal dish) and a Makgeolli, a rice beer that tastes like cantaloupe. The chickens cooked by the chef are slaughtered that very morning [36 W 26th St].

The neighborhood is also home to **Hangawi**, one of the best vegetarian restaurants in the city. Here, you'll eat in a zen atmosphere, sitting on the floor without shoes on [12 E 32nd St]. I also like **Mandoo Bar** where they hand-make dumplings in front of the restaurant's window, for passersby to see [2 W 32nd St].

To feel out of my element in my own city, I opt for **Gaonnuri** nestled on the 39th floor of an office tower. The restaurant, whose name means "center of the world" in Korean, has a spectacular view of Herald Square's illuminated buildings. Each table has its own barbecue in the middle; it's the perfect spot for group dinners or a birthday celebration [1250 Broadway].

The New Hip Neighborhood

150

In the last few years, a new neighborhood has popped up in Manhattan. The mostly unappealing section of Broadway between 23rd and 30th streets was nicknamed the "nameless rectangle" up until recently. It was the neighborhood of counterfeit perfume, suitcase and wig sellers. The area was renamed **NoMad** in 2010 (an acronym of NOrth of MADison Square Park). The arrival of many start-ups, the **Ace Hotel**, **Opening Ceremony** boutique, **Stumptown Coffee Roasters**, as well as restaurants **The Breslin** and **John Dory Oyster Bar**—all located at the corner of Broadway and 29th Street—has revitalized the neighborhood.

A New Yorker favorite, the famous **Rizzoli Bookstore**, decided to set down roots in the district after spending 50 years in Midtown [1133 Broadway].

My favorite restaurant in this part of town is **Marta** (A), a pizzeria that set up shop in **Martha Washington Hotel**'s grand lobby. I take a seat at the bar and watch chef Nick Anderer at work. His thin-crust, crispy rustic pizzas are baked in wood-burning ovens. Meat, fish and vegetables are roasted over embers in the Roman tradition [29 E 29th St].

At the corner of Broadway and 28th Street, **The NoMad Hotel** (B) is reminiscent of the Costes de Paris hotel with its atrium, thick velvet drapes, gilding, library, claw-foot bathtubs, dark lobby and restaurant that's popular with fashionistas. French interior designer Jacques Garcia decorated both hotels. Some of NoMad's rooms were actually inspired by his Parisian apartment. The 1905 beaux-arts-style building was entirely restored, and its facade looks like the magnificent buildings of Haussmann Boulevard in Paris. Maison Kitsuné has actually opened its first shop outside of Paris on their ground floor [1170 Broadway].

150 A

150 B

151

Wells in the Sky

151 New York has its **water towers**. They're a part of the scenery, much like the Statue of Liberty and the Empire State Building, but few people are aware of their actual purpose. It's estimated that there are approximately 10,000 towers on rooftops in Manhattan, especially on the south part of the island. Each one contains enough water to supply a building for a day. In the 19th century, authorities forced buildings of more than six floors to install these reservoirs because the water pressure from municipal aqueducts wasn't strong enough to supply the upper floors. That's still the case today, since the infrastructure has yet to be updated.

New York's drinking water—some of the best in the world—is carried by way of gravity from basins in northern parts of the state. During the summer, the municipality hooks up drinking fountains directly to fire hydrants, from which pedestrians can quench their thirst.

The Temple of Avant-Garde Fashion

152 London's fashion mecca, **Dover Street Market**, opened a location in New York in January 2014 in Murray Hill, a neighborhood that might be the least fashionable in Manhattan. The multi-level complex—laid out like an old bank—showcases the creations of renowned designers, including Prada and Comme des Garçons, as well as many emerging ones. The clothes are all exorbitantly priced; I visit this place to find out about trends and to eat at **Rose Bakery**, the popular Parisian restaurant on the ground floor. Co-owner Rose Carrarini is British, so they serve tea with scones after 4 p.m., along with coffee, wines, and fresh fruit juices [160 Lexington Ave].

The Library of Precious Books

153 If you like books, architecture and history, you have to visit the impressive **Pierpont Morgan Library** at least once in your lifetime. In 1906, the rich financial analyst and bibliophile commissioned the building of an annex to his house to store his impressive collection of books and old objects. The building is inspired by the architecture of Italian Renaissance villas. You can see a cast of George Washington's face made in 1785, some of Mozart's sheet music, a Gutenberg bible printed in 1445, letters from Thomas Jefferson to his daughter and 25 original excerpts of the United States Declaration of Independence [225 Madison Ave].

I ♥ NY

154 Octogenarian Milton Glaser is the creator of the famous I ♥ NY logo. Born in the Bronx to a father who was a tailor, Milton speaks fondly of his hometown: "It's a city that is hungry for ideas. It's not a place, it's a state of mind—a screen on which ideas can be projected."

After 60 years of work, he still runs his graphic design business. Surrounded by the next generation of young talent working away at computers, Milton Glaser presides, old-fashioned pencil in hand. Curiously, the famous logo is nowhere to be seen, except on a tiny pin. When asked to recount the origins of the logo, Mr. Glaser lets out a sigh, "For me, this story is quite boring..." he says, sitting in his office in the same building where he founded *New York Magazine* in 1968.

In the 1970s, the State of New York asked him to come up with an advertising campaign to bring tourists to the city. New York was going through a major fiscal crisis, residents and businesses were fleeing the city, crime and drug trafficking were on the rise, and the streets were littered with dog droppings. In short, New York had no glamor. Many argue that the little red and black logo, designed in 1977, in some ways saved the Big Apple. "It's rather pretentious of me to say this, but in a certain way it's true, because it crystallized New Yorkers' love for their city. At the time, people were not proud of their city at all, but wearing this logo created a shift in opinion."

The idea for the logo came to him in a taxi. "My first design was very banal: two diamonds with the words *I love New York*. I was in a taxi one night and thought to myself that I could do better. So I wrote on a scrap of paper *I ♥ NY*. It's hardly a work of genius," he says modestly.

He is still baffled by the success of these four simple characters. "It's incomprehensible. I can't leave the house without seeing it. It's so pervasive it's become invisible."

Why does he think the logo has resonated with so many? "Because it's a sequence of three small pieces of a puzzle: the 'I' is a personal pronoun; the 'NY' is an abbreviation of a city; and the heart symbolizes emotion. The message has to be decoded, which etches it in people's minds. But the real explanation is that I have no idea."

Today, it is said that all of the products bearing the logo generate a total of $30 million a year. Mr. Glaser has never seen a penny of it, since he agreed to develop the logo free of charge as a way to help his city. Despite this, he has no hard feelings. "I didn't do it for the money, and in any case, it would be difficult to quantify its value. I've earned a lot of money in my career, and I can afford not to worry about it."

The logo has made a comeback since September 11, 2001. "The day after the attacks, I realized that I Love New York was no longer enough after what had happened. I just realized that I loved my city more than ever. Like when someone gets sick, you realize just how much you love them." Mr. Glaser created a poster with a new version, *I ♥ New York More Than Ever*, with a black spot on the heart representing Ground Zero.

"We printed five thousand posters, and about sixty students put them up all over the city. New Yorkers responded very well because our efforts were sincere, it wasn't advertising." Today, the posters can still be seen in some store windows.

It was also Milton Glaser who designed the imagery for the legendary Windows on the World restaurant that was perched atop of the North Tower of the World Trade Center. In his office, he has a shelf where the remaining plates and cups from the restaurant are displayed.

Has New York fully recovered from the tragedy? "The psychological wound is deep and has not yet healed," he replies. "But good things have come from it. I think the city has become aware of the fragility of things. New Yorkers have stopped taking their city for granted."

Candy Cab

155

During my time in New York, you might say that I've had a full spectrum of taxi experiences (one driver, on drugs, brought me to New Jersey against my will, another stopped to pray mid-route). Every cab ride is an adventure. But Mansoor Khalid, also known as **Candy Cab**, takes the cake.

Originally from Pakistan, Mansoor came to New York in 1993 and got an engineering degree. As is often the case in New York, he could not find gainful employment in his field, so he started driving a taxi part-time to supplement his income. About 10 years ago, he made it his full-time job.

On April 12, 2012, Mansoor experienced a great tragedy: his only son Saad, who was 18 months old, died from complications related to a congenital heart defect. Every night after his shift, he would visit his son at a hospital in the Bronx. He always brought coffees and cakes to the nurses and doctors, who soon nicknamed him "coffee man." Seeing the smiles on their faces brought him some comfort.

When he returned to work after the death of his son, he wanted to continue this new tradition and decided to offer treats to his customers. Today, Mansoor spends an average of $300 per week on bags of candy.

"My taxi is like my second wife. I take care of it." A sign in the cab reads: NO EATING OR DRINKING IN THIS CAR—EXCEPT CANDIES. The ledge below the rear window is filled with sweets, and every time he brakes, licorice and lollipops rain down on the passenger seat. His trunk is fully stocked, and he keeps a bag of chocolate in front. He encourages his customers to eat it all.

"The first day I did this, the candy was gone within a few hours. I realized that this could change someone's day. Since then, I've never stopped offering candy to my customers." He also installed disco lights and speakers in the passenger area so that customers can listen to music on their iPhones.

"To me, it's like a business card, and I have my Twitter, Facebook and Instagram accounts," he told me. And he has thousands of followers. You can contact him on Twitter (@candycabNYC) and he promises to pick you up at no extra charge. And if it's your birthday, the ride is free.

Through word of mouth, Mansoor Khalid has become a local celebrity, and some customers are especially moved by his extreme generosity, which is hard to come by in a big city like New York. After reading his story online, one customer sent him a PayPal link for $300.

After spending 20 minutes in his taxi, I came away with my hands full of candy and a smile on my face.

Neon Lights, Big Avenues and Broadway

Midtown, Long Island City

177
W 70TH ST
HHP
AMSTERDAM
W 62ND ST
W 61ST ST
W 60TH ST
W 59TH ST
CENTRAL PARK SOUTH
• 178
W 58TH ST
189
W 57TH ST
CARNEGIE HALL
W 56TH ST
182 • 184
BROADWAY
W 55TH ST • 176
182 •
W 54TH ST
10TH AVE
182
7TH AVE
AVE OF THE AMERICAS
W 53RD ST
182
W 52ND ST
• 176
182
W 51ST ST
9TH AVE
176
MIDTOWN
11TH AVE
W 49TH ST
• 176
W 48TH ST
W 48TH ST
• 176
8TH AVE
• 176
• 176
6TH AVE
W 46TH ST
• 170
W 45TH ST
167 •
176 •
W 44TH ST
176 •
10TH AVE
168
176
W 43RD ST
W 42ND ST
158 •
W 41ST ST
156 •
BROADWAY
W 40TH ST
W 40TH ST
W 39TH ST
7TH AVE
6TH AVE
W 38TH ST
DYER ST
W 37TH ST
9TH AVE
8TH AVE
W 36TH ST
W 35TH ST
W 34TH ST
W 33RD ST
• 172

Legend:
- ● Sights + photo ops
- ● Bars + restaurants
- ● Stores + markets
- ● Arts + culture
- ● Activities + walks

The Library Chock-Full of Treasures

156 A trip to the **New York Public Library** is a must, if only to see the frescoes on the ceiling of the 3rd floor reading room (the Rose Main Reading Room). I often go there to write and find inspiration. In the room across the hall (the Edna Barnes Salomon Room), you can work surrounded by paintings of George Washington, the Astor family and other notorious characters, including writer Truman Capote. This is one of those New York public spaces, much like the hall of Grand Central Station, that ennobles the everyday lives of the city's citizens. Opened in 1911, the beaux-arts-style library is home to nearly 15 million works, including a copy of the Gutenberg Bible and medieval manuscripts. There's even a collection of rare baseball cards and 45,000 restaurant menus that date back to the 1800s. The majority of the books are stored underground in two gigantic rooms dug beneath Bryant Park. Access to the library is free, as is the Wi-Fi. You'll be greeted by Patience and Courage, the two marble lions that guard the building's entrance [5th Ave and 42nd St].

The impressive **Kinokuniya** bookstore located on the other side of the park is also a well of inspiration. Open in New York since the 1980s, this place stocks 20,000 Japanese books, as wells as English ones and a huge selection of fashion, architecture and design magazines [1073 6th Ave].

The Gallery Tour

157 **The Fuller Building**, a magnificent Art Deco structure (1929), houses many art galleries that are open to the public. The lobby itself is worth the trip. I often attend the **Howard Greenberg Gallery**'s exhibits that specialize in photography (14th floor). It's the perfect place to escape Midtown's tumult.

I'm an admirer of Vivian Maier, the street photographer whose work was discovered after her death. Howard Greenberg is the only gallery in the United States that showcases and sells her photos.

The gallery also exhibits shots by Eugène Atget, Henri Cartier-Bresson and New Yorker Joel Meyerowitz—one of my favorite street photographers [41 E 57th St]. Ask for the galleries directory at reception.

After a visit, I often recharge at **Menkui-Tei**, a Japanese hole-in-the-wall that's not much to look at, but serves many delicious ramen soups for a few bucks each [60 W 56th St].

Green Sculptures from Quebec

158 At the corner of 6th Avenue and 42nd Street, have a look at the atrium of **Bank of America**'s headquarters. You'll see four plant-based sculptures that were designed for Montreal's Mosaïcultures Internationales. One of them is 7.5 meters (25 feet) tall and weighs 25 tons. The lobby's design was inspired by Tim Burton's movies [115 W 42nd St].

159

An Oasis Between the Skyscrapers

159 **Bryant Park**, behind the library, is one of the most beautiful parks in New York. You can skate there during the winter, but I prefer going in the summer for the outdoor library, old merry-go-round, and bocce ball and ping-pong players. You can pick a spot to work outside, since there are about 40 electrical outlets for computers and free Wi-Fi access. If you want to have a picnic, know that the restaurant across the street, **Le Pain Quotidien**, sells takeout meals [70 W 40th St], while **Untamed Sandwiches** makes delicious grilled vegetable or braised meat sandwiches [43 W 39th St].

Italian Delicacies at Small Prices

160 For coffee worthy of its name and quality lunches just a few steps away from Grand Central Station, I go to **Cipriani Le Specialità**. They sell pastries, sandwiches, pasta and salads at affordable prices, a rare find in the business district. Many Italians patronize this cafe, which is a good sign. Have a seat outside and watch the parade of passersby [110 E 42nd St].

The Whispering Gallery

161

Here's Grand Central Terminal's worst kept secret, but still one of its most romantic ones. In front of the Oyster Bar's entrance, a large vault upheld by two arches has mysterious acoustic properties. When two people stand at either end of it, they can whisper and hear each other. Many people take advantage of the **Whispering Gallery**'s magic for marriage proposals.

Oysters Beneath the Vault

162

Founded in 1913, the **Grand Central Oyster Bar** in Grand Central Station hasn't been forgotten by New Yorkers, even if it's very touristy. It's especially obvious at lunch when Midtown's businessmen roll in. Enjoying oysters in Grand Central is classic New York. I love this seafood restaurant for its cafeteria vibe, vaulted tile ceilings, and red and white checked tablecloths. Along with the traditional dining room, the restaurant has a "saloon" section and sandwich counter. They always sell 30 or so types of oysters and excellent Florida key lime pie. Some oysters go for $1.25 a piece from 4:30 p.m. to 7 p.m. [89 E 42nd St].

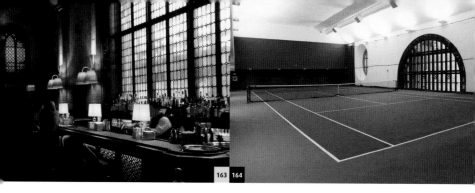

163 164

The Apartment-Bar

163

The Campbell Apartment is an amazing bar located in John W. Campbell's old office. The rich businessman rented this part of Grand Central Station in the 1920s. It was his office by day and a bar where he hosted friends by night. To design the decor, he gleaned inspiration from 18th century Florentine palaces. People say he spent $300,000 on the Persian rugs alone [15 Vanderbilt Ave].

Playing Tennis While Waiting for the Train

164

Grand Central Terminal is probably the only station in the world where you can play tennis. The **Vanderbilt Tennis Club** on the 4th floor has two tennis courts that are open to the public. You can glimpse Park Avenue through the arched windows. You'll find it by going through the door at 15 Vanderbilt Avenue and then taking the elevator. You need to reserve a court a week in advance by e-mailing the following address: desk@ vanderbilttennisclub.com.

Like in Tokyo

165

To get away from tourist routes in New York, sometimes you need to scratch beneath the surface. The izakaya (sake bar offering small Japanese dishes) **Sagakura** is located in the basement of an unremarkable office building. To get there, you must go through the lobby, say hello to the security guard and go down the stairs. At the end of the concrete hallway, there's an unexpected dining room. Even the bathrooms are high-tech like in Tokyo. They serve nearly 200 kinds of sake [211 E 43rd St]. On the other side of the street, you'll find one of the most reputed sushi restaurants in town, **Yasuda** [204 E 43rd St].

A taxi is free when their middle lantern light is on. If the two sidelights are on, the taxi is off duty (you'll see these words). If all the lantern lights are off, it means the taxi is occupied. #onlyinNY

The Urban Enclave

166 Strolling down the north side of East 42nd Street, east of 2nd Avenue, you'll find a flight of stairs that goes up into a distinct neighborhood, Tudor City. It's a Tudor-style (some would call it neo-Gothic), 12-building complex from the 1920s. Isolated from the urban grid, it's a place where you can go to escape the city's chaos. I love walking around its parks with a very English design. They actually filmed scenes from *Spider-Man* at 5 Tudor City Place. When retracing your steps, don't miss the art deco **Daily News Building** with its giant globe [220 E 42nd St], as well as the tropical gardens open to the public in the atrium of the **Ford Foundation Building**. It's a small, green jungle at the heart of the concrete jungle [320 E 43rd St, or access from 42nd St].

Times Square, the Zen Way

167 On Broadway between 45th and 46th streets, on the central pedestrian island, there's a subway airshaft. Soft, mysterious harmonies float up through the vent's metal grate. I lived in this neighborhood for two years when I first arrived in New York, and I wondered for a long time where these sounds came from. I finally found out that they were the product of a sound sculpture hidden by American artist Max Nehaus (died in 2009) in the air vents in 1977. There's no plaque marking its presence, it's therefore up to passersby to discover the installation. The piece called **Times Square** creates a meditative atmosphere in the very heart of one of the most chaotic places on Earth.

Broadway's Pantheon

168

Located right in the middle of the theater district, **Sardi's** has been closely bound to the theater world since the 1920s. It's in this restaurant that the idea for creating the Tony Awards—the Oscars of the theater—came about, and the walls are covered with nearly 1,200 caricatures of actors. The original works are kept in a safe, and reproductions are hung up throughout the dining room.

Italian immigrants Melchiore Pio Vincenzo Sardi and Eugenia Pallera met as they arrived at Ellis Island in 1907. They got married and opened their first restaurant in 1921 before establishing Sardi's in 1927. When Mr. Sardi passed away in 1969, his son Vincent took control of the restaurant. A theater lover, Vincent always seated out-of-work actors next to tables with producers. There was also a special blackboard for broke actors. After his death in 2007, over 600 unpaid bills were found. They still have a discounted menu for actors to this day, and employees receive free tickets to Broadway musicals.

Sardi's golden age was in the 1960s. On opening nights, the atmosphere in the dining room after a show was a kind of barometer that indicated the play's success or failure. Shortly after midnight, the first freshly printed copies of the New York Times and New York Herald Tribune were delivered to the restaurant. Patrons wasted no time before reading the reviews. If they were negative, a weighted silence descended upon the room. If it was positive, there was champagne for everyone.

After all these years, this spot hasn't lost any of its soul. You might be served by an employee who's been working there for 50 years, or find yourself seated next to nonagenarian William Herz eating at table 4, just as it's been on every Tuesday for the last 80 years. They serve him his coffee in the same old white cup that's stowed away in the back room until he returns [234 W 44th St].

Bloody Mary and Old New York

169 For a drink in a very old New York ambiance, I recommend the St. Regis Hotel's **King Cole Bar** (A). Marilyn Monroe, Joe DiMaggio, John Lennon and Salvador Dali were all regulars. This is the bar where the Bloody Mary was invented. Parisian barman Fernand Petiot brought the recipe with him to New York in 1934, and it was an instant success with customers. Since the name was too vulgar for the hotel, the cocktail was renamed the Red Snapper. It's still their specialty to this day. The *Old King Cole* mural behind the bar is famous. Painted by artist Maxfield Parrish, people say it hides a secret. You'll have to get on the waiters' good side to find out what it is. Don't miss the bellhop and valet cabin in front of the hotel; it's over 100 years old and looks like a copper submarine [2 E 55th St].

Another option is the **Bar Room** at restaurant **21 Club**. The establishment opened its doors in 1929, while Prohibition was in full swing. The clandestine bar had a fall system to hide alcohol bottles when the police arrived. With the years, the bar became a meeting spot for American presidents, Wall Street's high rollers, Hollywood stars and news anchors. I love the ceiling covered in hanging toys donated by loyal customers throughout the years. Men have to wear a jacket [21 W 52nd St].

Back to New York in the Roaring Twenties

170 Watching a performance of *Queen of the Night* is a bit like being in a Baz Luhrmann movie. An evening in what was once the Diamond Horseshoe—a cabaret buried in the Paramount Hotel's basement in Midtown—feels like New York has gone back to the 1920s.

Vaguely inspired by Mozart's opera *The Magic Flute*, *Queen of the Night* is produced by Randy Weiner, the genius behind *Sleep No More*, another successful show that's been staged in New York since 2011 (see reason No. 115).

It's at once an immersive play, opera, dance, circus and magic show, as well as a gastronomical experience.

This show breaks the fourth wall between spectators and actors. Performers come and take you by the hand to make you dance, kiss your neck and lead you into secret rooms. The show is very sexy without being vulgar.

The accompanying banquet is gargantuan. Alcohol flows freely, and the waiters' dance—parading with platters of lobster and suckling pig—is spectacular. Tickets cost $125, and you should reserve your seat ahead of time [235 W 46th St].

169 A

ST REGIS

171

Diamond Street

171 They call 47th Street between 5th and 6th avenues the **Diamond District**. About 2,000 jewelers compete on this stretch of street. Even if you're not looking for a ring, it's fascinating to watch this typically New York display. They say that 90% of all the diamonds that arrive in the United States pass through 47th Street. You might see Raffi Stepanian down on all fours on the sidewalk. The Queens resident makes a living by picking up fallen diamond and ruby fragments, as well as chains and earrings with a pair of tweezers. He claims to make about $500 a week.

Electronic Paradise

172 If you're in the market for a new camera, or photo and video equipment, **B&H** has been patronized by New Yorkers for 40 years. It's the largest independent electronics store in the United States, and they serve nearly 5,000 people a day. The purchasing process is unique: the chosen item moves through an elaborate system of bins and conveyor belts, and you only pick it up at the exit. The owner and about 300 of the employees are Hasidic Jews, so the store closes at around 2 p.m. on Friday, as Saturday is Shabbat. Between the thousands of in-store customers, and many more online, B&H has more than 5,000 employees [420 9th Ave].

The Culinary Far West

173 **Gotham West Market** was established in 2014 on 11th Avenue, a deserted part of town that will be completely transformed in the next few years thanks to Hudson Yards real estate development. This food court counts stalls from all over the world, including **Slurp Shop**, reputed chef Ivan Orkin's ramen bar. I also recommend the tapas bar **El Colmado** where they serve Catalonian wine.

Don: Shoe Shiner Extraordinaire

174 You can't walk by the corner of 47th Street and 6th Avenue in Manhattan without being beckoned by Don Ward, the Midtown shoe shiner. His sales technique is a blend of arrogance, improvisation and humor that is typically New York. "Sir, do you want to keep your job? It sure doesn't look like it with those shoes." "Do you think you can get ahead in this life, young man? Take a look at your shoes. It's the details that matter!" "Hey man! If you like your Doc Martens, prove it to me!"

Most people ignore him and keep walking, examining their shoes with some embarrassment when they get a bit farther away. Sometimes, however, the situation escalates: He has had a customer spit on him and another swing at his face with a briefcase. But in general, the technique works. Don polishes up to 60 pairs of shoes a day, five days a week. In his 22-year career, he has shined nearly 700,000 shoes. He says he will stop at one

million. One day, when he shouted at a man to look at how dirty his shoes were, the man answered: "Look at your own shoes!" Sure enough, his own shoes were no cleaner. "I promised myself that would never happen again," Don told me. "Now I shine my shoes every morning, before my cup of coffee."

Rain or snow, Don Ward leaves his home in the Bronx at dawn to set up his stand and two chairs at the same intersection he has been at for 15 years.

"One day," Don recounted, "a man asked me what my biggest tip was. I told him a hundred dollars. He said, "Here's a hundred-and-one dollars. Now I'm your biggest tip." Don is probably one the happiest shoe shiners out there. "I love what I do. I smile all the time. I love the freedom. I'm the employee and the boss. This stand isn't a pedestal, it's my work tool."

Now that I live in the south of the island, I don't see Don as much as I used to, but sometimes I ride my bike up 6th Avenue just to hear his voice. His energy is contagious. If you ever go there, tell him "Merie" sent you.

The Real Kramer

175

What could be more typically New York than going for coffee at a diner with the real Kramer? **Kenny Kramer** is the New Yorker who inspired the famous character in the cult TV series *Seinfeld*. The life of the real Kramer, 73 years old in 2016, took a new turn in 1977 when he moved into a subsidized housing complex in the Hell's Kitchen neighborhood, where he still lives today. At the time, he was far from suspecting that his neighbor Larry David, co-creator of *Seinfeld*, would one day use him as inspiration for the character of Cosmo Kramer.

While the similarities between the real Kramer and the fictional character are striking, there is a crucial difference: "I don't burst through the door like a whirlwind," explained Kenny Kramer, whose long gray hair shows that he is still a hippie at heart.

Kenny and Larry lived across the hall from each other for six years. Just like in the TV series, they would leave their doors open and go from one apartment to the other. "Except in real life," Kenny explained, "the food was at my place." The two have remained friends ever since.

When Jerry Seinfeld contacted Larry David in 1988 to collaborate on his NBC series, David tapped into the absurdity of his everyday life. "For example," Kenny explained, "we really did ask the Chinese delivery guy to help us order a cure for baldness. Like on the show, we filmed Larry's head so we could compare later. I still have the tape. We were also banned from the fruit stand on the corner. Everything in the episode is true."

Before agreeing to the project, Larry David asked for his neighbor's permission. "I said yes, as long as they would hire me as an actor." Unfortunately, NBC executives refused, offering him a fee instead. "I can't disclose the amount, because it's confidential, but it wasn't much," Kenny explained.

In retrospect, he recognizes that casting Michael Richards in the part was a wise choice. "I would never have been as good as him. He added a very physical aspect to the character."

The public was introduced to Kenny through a *Rolling Stone* article published in 1991.

"After that, a reporter from the *New York Post* went to the library to look through old telephone directories from the seventies and found me."

In the 1990s, Kenny could receive thousands of calls per week for interviews, especially after the *New York Times* published his personal number 1-800-KRAMERS, which he had been using as a "chick magnet" in New York bars.

Born in the Bronx, Kenny describes himself as a product of the psychedelic revolution of the 1960s: "I'm really good at doing nothing," he explained. He left

"I don't burst through the door like a whirlwind."

school at the age of 17, sold magazines door to door, was a drummer in a band, and a stand-up comic, among other things, but it was his line of bright disco jewelry that made him a fortune—a classic "Kramer" idea.

In 1997, he even ran for Mayor of New York. "I had some crazy ideas, like giving free phones to schizophrenics so they wouldn't scare tourists by talking to nobody." He got 1,408 votes running against Michael Bloomberg's $78-million campaign.

Twenty years ago, Kenny started offering guided tours—The Kramer Reality Tour—taking *Seinfeld* fans to sites made famous on the show. Reality meets fiction in the streets of New York.

Hell's Kitchen

176

I steer clear of Times Square restaurants; most are tourist traps. I prefer to opt for eateries in **Hell's Kitchen**, a neighborhood that owes its name to its past as a criminal stronghold.

Thanks to his Neapolitan pizza, **Don Antonio** is a Midtown institution. The chef Antonio Starita is also the owner of one of the oldest and most venerated pizzerias in Naples, Starita, founded in 1901. The menu lists 60 different types of pizza. Try the Pizza del Papa (the Pope's pizza!) and the one topped with pistachio pesto, Italian sausage and mozzarella. They also serve dessert pizza with a slightly fried crust [309 W 50th St].

For ramen soup like in Tokyo, I head to **Totto Ramen**, a small counter with 10 seats [366 W 52nd St]. For a meal on the go, I like the dim sum at **Kung Fu Little Steamed Buns Ramen**. You can watch young Chinese chef Peter Song making the noodles while dancing behind the window [811 8th Ave].

Another of the neighborhood's well-kept secrets is wine and cheese bar **Kashkaval Garden**. They serve meat and cheese platters, a large selection of tapas, soups, salads, cheese fondue and inexpensive wine [852 9th Ave].

For lunch to go, I like to stop in at **Amy's Bread** for sandwiches [672 9th Ave], **Poseidon Greek Bakery** for baklava and spanakopita [629 9th Ave] and **Sullivan Street Bakery** for focaccia [533 W 47th].

On show nights, Thai restaurant **Room Service** is ideal for their very speedy service. Don't be put off by the tacky, very 2000s decor [690 9th Ave].

When I'm in the mood for a sophisticated meal in Times Square, I go to **Lambs Club**, established in an old theater club that used to be visited by Fred Astaire and Charlie Chaplin. In this art deco setting, you'll feel as if you're in one of Broadway's old speakeasies. It's also a good spot for a pre-show drink [132 W 44th St].

The Polo Bar—designer Ralph Lauren's restaurant—is worth the trip if only to admire the equestrian-inspired decor. This place has great elegance, they serve American cuisine classics, the service is very attentive and you might spot a celebrity or two [1 E 55th St].

Avoid Little Italy and Times Square's restaurants at all costs. #onlyinNY

Riverside Park

177

After your meal, why not go for a stroll along the bike bath by the Hudson River? North of West 58th Street, the park becomes wilder. There's ship wreckage, willow trees, a marina at West 79th Street, docks with lounge chairs and a spectacular view of the George Washington Bridge. A great place for a picnic and to escape the city's brouhaha.

The Terra-Cotta Castle

178

Some of Manhattan's buildings are beautiful enough to take your breath away. That's the case with **Alwyn Court**, a treasure of early 20th-century New York architecture. Classified as a historical monument since 1966, the investment building reminds me of a huge terra-cotta wedding cake. The famous, chic caviar restaurant **Petrossian** has set up shop on the ground floor [180 W 58th St].

Don't be afraid of the white smoke that wafts up from the sidewalks and streets. It's simply water vapor escaping from fissures in underground pipes. Most of the city's plumbing is from the early 20th century, and breakage is common. #onlyinNY

The Accessories Mecca

179 Fifth Avenue counts **Henri Bendel** among its great stores. This place was founded in 1895 by the man who would be the first to import Coco Chanel's creations to the United States. The store that now focuses exclusively on accessories is the ideal place to discover the newest trendy jewelry and handbag lines, and to try out beauty products and perfume. The store spans four floors. Don't miss the powder rooms in the basement [712 5th Ave].

If you're crazy about shoes, make sure to check out the impressive **Shoe Salon** one block north, on the second floor of the **Bergdorf Goodman** store. It's designer-shoe heaven. Most of them are incredibly expensive, but nothing can keep you from dreaming [754 5th Ave].

Drinking in Front of the Empire State Building

180 If you want to take photos of the Empire State Building, one of the most beautiful views of it is on the **Strand Hotel**'s roof. The **Top of the Strand** bar's terrace is open to the public, and is a good place to stop in for a cocktail and a bite to eat, both during the day and at night [33 W 37th St].

If you want to look at a map or your phone when on the sidewalk, don't stop suddenly: That's the best way to upset a New Yorker in a hurry. Instead, step off to the side near the buildings. #onlyinNY

Marilyn Monroe's Subway Grate

181 The famous grate that lifted up the legendary actress' white dress in the film *The Seven Year Itch* is located at the corner of **Lexington Avenue** and **52nd Street**. Director Billy Wilder had placed a fan beneath the grate. Filmed on a brisk September evening in 1954, the scene attracted almost 1,500 onlookers and photographers. Some say that it was a way to promote the movie, since this scene was reshot in a studio. Regardless, the photos of Marilyn on the subway grate became icons of American culture. Sixty years later, a French bistro replaced the jewelry store in the background. The boss told me "one day, a man came to visit the grate. He needed tissues he was crying so much."

180

Secret Passages Between the Avenues

182

London's King's Cross station has its 9 ¾ platform, and Manhattan has 6 ½ Avenue. Believe it or not, it's actually a pedestrian walkway that connects 51st and 57th streets, passing through a series of galleries, atriums, hallways and building lobbies. You'll find its southern entrance between 6th and 7th avenues. The City of New York has even made traffic signs that read "**6 ½ Av.**"

Woody Allen's Manhattan

183

To feel like you're in *Manhattan*, the famous director's cult film, have a seat on a bench at the lookout on the easternmost side of **East 58th Street** (at the corner of Riverview Terrace and Sutton Square). The famous scene with Woody Allen and Diane Keaton was filmed at four in the morning in August 1978. The City of New York agreed to keep the Queensboro Bridge's lights on for the shoot.

The Snack Bar in a Chic Hotel

184

Hidden behind a thick velvet curtain in the Parker Meridian Hotel's lobby, **Burger Joint** is an authentic greasy spoon. The dark snack bar with fake-wood-paneled walls scribbled over with graffiti whips up excellent milkshakes, fries and burgers. The entrance is beneath the neon sign in the shape of... a hamburger [119 W 56th St].

Salvation Burger, celebrity chef April Bloomfield's restaurant, also serves excellent hamburgers in a Midtown hotel, the **Pod 51** [230 E 51st St].

Bring your Own Wine... to the MoMA

186 The **Museum of Modern Art**, one of New York's greatest museums (my favorite), also houses one of the best restaurants in town. Here's a little-known trick for eating at the Modern without breaking the bank: On Sundays, the restaurant allows customers to bring their own wine into the bar section (no more than two bottles per table). It's best to mention it when making the reservation [9 W 53rd St]. If you check out the museum in the summer, there are jazz concerts in the sculpture garden [MoMA.org/summergarden].

185

The King of New York Barmen

185 Doug Quinn is a New York legend. Many call him "the barman of your dreams." Seeing him waltz around behind his counter is a delight. He mixes a dozen cocktails at a time, while keeping an eye on the door. His phenomenal memory is what impresses me most. Tell him your name once and he'll remember it the next time. He'll also remember what you drink. Regulars, who he affectionately calls "sweet peach," barely set foot inside and their drink is waiting at the bar. He dresses in pastels and wears a different bow tie every day. Doug Quinn is also an amazing matchmaker. His philosophy? "A good barman can find you a date for the night, a new job and an apartment." After spending 10 years at P.J. Clarke's, he opened his own bar, **Hudson Malone**, named after his two sons [218 E 53rd St].

Sunset Between the Skyscrapers

187 "**Manhattanhenge**" is a phenomenon that occurs twice a year (in May and July) when the setting sun aligns perfectly with the east-west axis of Manhattan's street grid. For a few minutes, the city is bathed in golden light and New Yorkers turn toward the Hudson River. These are magical moments.

Popular New York astrophysicist Neil deGrasse Tyson coined the term "Manhattanhenge" in 2002. It derives from the names Manhattan and Stonehenge, the famous megalithic monument in the south of England. To get the best photos, you simply need to head to 14th, 23rd, 34th or 42nd streets just before sunset. A guaranteed Instagram success.

A Piece of German History in Midtown

188

Few people know it, but you can see five intact panels of the **Berlin Wall** in the office building located at 520 Madison Avenue. It used to sit outside the building, but had to be removed for conservation purposes in 2014 before finding a new home in the building's lobby in 2015. The property owner bought the relics in 1990 and had them shipped to New York at a high cost. The wall's old western facade is covered with graffiti by German artists Thierry Noir and Kiddy Citny. As for the eastern side, it's devoid of any inscription: a scathing reminder of the old communist regime of East Germany.

Gourmet Adventures a Stone's Throw from Central Park

189

The Plaza and the Waldorf Astoria are the only hotels classified as historical monuments. Built in 1907 to dethrone the St. Regis, The Plaza cost $12.5 million at the time. The inauguration of the neo-Renaissance-style castle marked the beginning of 5th Avenue's transformation into a commercial thoroughfare. To think that when they opened, a room went for $2.50!

To take advantage of The Plaza's amenities without spending a fortune, visit the food hall in the basement where many counters are lined with wine and cheese, frozen yogurt, sandwiches, macarons, cakes, pastries, sushi and seafood [1 W 59th St].

If you really want to treat yourself, they serve English tea beneath the **Palm Court** hotel's glass roof (A). This room reminds me of the *Titanic*'s interior. The service costs $65 per person (the "New Yorker Tea" menu), which includes tea, pastries and finger sandwiches. For $105 (the "Champagne Tea" menu), the sandwiches are turned up a notch with *foie gras*, smoked salmon, crab, lobster or sturgeon caviar, and they serve you a glass of Veuve Clicquot or Moët & Chandon.

They also serve tea at **The Russian Tea Room** (B), a mythic New York establishment open for almost 90 years. Madonna even worked the coatroom in 1982, and they filmed many movie scenes there, like ones from *When Harry Met Sally*. The service costs $50, which is more than enough for two people [150 W 57th St].

An Elevated Day in Manhattan

190 People often ask me where to see the best view of New York, to which I reply the **"Top of the Rock"** without hesitation. After being closed for 25 years, the Rockefeller Center's observatory reopened in 2005 after $75 million in renovations. The ticket costs $29, but it's worth it if only for snapping breathtaking photos of Manhattan. On the 70th floor, the view spreads out for 130 kilometers (80 miles) all around. It's totally clear, unlike what can be observed from the top of the Empire State Building. A tip: Go early to skip the hoards of tourists and wedding photo sessions. The observatory is open from 8 a.m. to midnight, seven days a week. The $42 Sun & Stars ticket allows you to check out the observatory twice in the same day: during the day and in the evening. Once night falls, the show is even more amazing [30 Rockefeller Plaza].

For unforgettable brunch, reserve a table at the **Rainbow Room**, the legendary art deco restaurant with a revolving dance floor up on the tower's 65th floor. Founded in 1934, it's been the setting of fabulous parties. It was the first restaurant established in a New York skyscraper. They're open on Monday nights for dinners with an orchestra ($175 per person) and for Sunday brunch ($95 per person). The gigantic buffet finds inspiration in cuisines from all over the world. It's best to reserve a table (rainbowroom.com). The **Sixtyfive** cocktail lounge, also on the 65th floor, is open Monday to Friday, from 5 p.m. to midnight [30 Rockefeller Plaza].

The Contemporary Art Neighborhood

191 Long Island City in Queens is one subway stop away from Grand Central Station in Manhattan. This neighborhood is chock-full of contemporary art galleries and unexpected treasures. I usually go to check out the exhibits at **PS1** (A), a branch of the Museum of Modern Art (MoMA). The museum was established in what was a public school that was over 100 years old [22-25 Jackson Ave]. Exhibits are very avant-garde and every Saturday of the summer, the schoolyard turns into a huge outdoor dance floor where DJs host the Warm Up series. After a visit to the museum, I stop in at **Mu Ramen** to eat one of their delicious soups. There's nothing more comforting [12-09 Jackson Ave].

You'll also find **The Cliffs** [11-11 44th Dr] in this neighborhood: an indoor climbing center of over 3,000 square meters (32,000 square feet). You can get to Long Island City by taking the 7, E and M trains [Court Square station].

Pied de Cochon's Influence in New York

192 Hugue Dufour and his wife Sarah Obraitis turned Long Island City into a new gourmet destination. The chef has attracted much praise from New York's press. His restaurant **M. Wells Dinette**, with a decor inspired by an old school cafeteria, is located in the MoMA PS1 museum [22-25 Jackson Ave]. The chef's second restaurant is a few blocks away in a repurposed garage. The **M. Wells Steakhouse** received its first Michelin star in October 2014. In the style of Montreal restaurant Pied de Cochon—where Hugue worked before moving to New York—servings are copious, dishes are surprising, and he's reinventing classics with panache [43-15 Crescent St].

191A

195

Unique Gardens

193 Who'd have thought? New York, the concrete jungle, is a leader in the urban agriculture world. Brooklyn Grange's huge vegetable garden grows on the roofs of two warehouses in Long Island City. It's open to the public every Saturday, from May to October. You can buy fresh produce or attend one of their banquets or yoga classes [37-18 Northern Blvd]. You can get there by subway, taking the M or R trains to 36th Street station.

Not far from there, you can visit the **Noguchi** museum's sculpture garden: a space so Zen you'll have a hard time believing you're still in New York. This museum was founded by the American-Japanese artist Isamu Noguchi (1904-1988). It's closed on Monday and Tuesday [9-01 33rd Rd].

A Greek Feast

194 After visiting the museum, head to one of the best Greek restaurants in New York, **Taverna Kyclades** in Astoria [33 07 Ditmars Blvd] 20 minutes away from the subway. After a good meal of grilled fish and lemon potatoes, enjoy their famous galaktoboureko, a dessert made with filo pastry and custard cream. The restaurant doesn't sell the dessert—it's on the house! You can get there by taking the N or Q trains to Astoria-Ditmars Boulevard station.

For the Love of Film

195 As it's slightly off the beaten tourist track, the **Museum of the Moving Image** is often forgotten. The museum is entirely dedicated to the history, aesthetics and techniques of cinema, television, video games and digital media. You'll find an impressive collection of old televisions and cameras, as well as many archived pieces like the Yoda puppet (*Star Wars*), the mask from *Mrs. Doubtfire* and the famous costume worn by Diane Keaton in *Annie Hall*. The museum is located in the old Kaufman Astoria studios where many movies were filmed in the 1920s, during the silent film era. The museum reopened in 2011 after $67 million worth of renovations [36-01 35th Ave]. To get there by subway from Manhattan, take the N/Q trains [36th Avenue station] or R/M [Steinway Street station].

S O L O M O N

The Big Museums and the City's Lungs

Upper East Side. Central Park

GUGGENHEIM MUSEUM

Upper East Side, Central Park

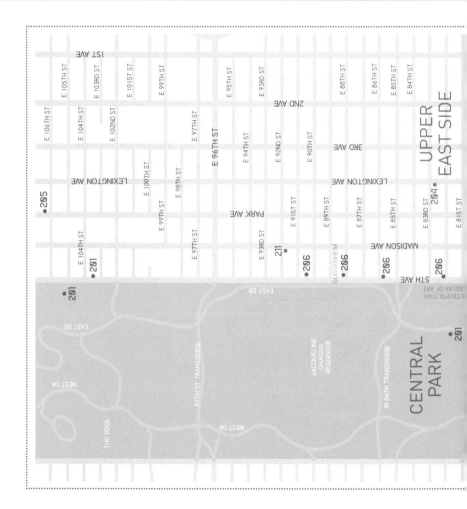

The Big Museums and the City's Lungs

Sights + photo ops
Bars + restaurants
Stores + markets
Arts + culture
Activities + walks

The Other Statue of Liberty

196 If you want to see the **Statue of Liberty**, but aren't in the mood to face the boat ride with hoards of tourists heading to Liberty Island, know that there's an exact replica of the figure in front of a Madison Avenue building. The three-meter (nine-foot) high figure was made with the original mold by French sculptor Auguste Bartholdi who designed the real statue. There are only 12 replicas of it in the world. Leonard Stern—the owner of the building—funded its production in honor of his father, an immigrant who arrived at Ellis Island from the Weimar Republic in 1926 and cried upon seeing the statue for the first time [667 Madison Ave].

196

The Millionaires' Street

197 The most beautiful houses in the Upper East Side are on 70th Street, between Lexington and Park Avenue. In 1939, *Fortune* magazine was already describing this stretch of street as the "**most beautiful block in New York**." It happens to be where Woody Allen lives.

Holly Golightly's House

198 One block farther north, you'll find the house of **Holly Golightly**, Audrey Hepburn's famous character from the film *Breakfast at Tiffany's*. It was sold for nearly $6 million in 2012 [169 E 71st St].

Woody Allen, the Clarinetist

199 It was the first outing I treated myself to when I got here; I wanted to live a typically New Yorker experience. For over 15 years, the famous filmmaker has played clarinet at **Cafe Carlyle** on Monday nights. He enters through the back door, always sits at the same table to assemble his instrument, and has a few words with his agent before going on stage where he plays with his musicians for an hour. He doesn't look at anyone and never emerges from his bubble. It feels more like attending a practice session with his garage band. That said, the evening is no bargain. You have to pay a $110 cover and drink for at least $25 worth just to sit at the bar [35 E 76th St].

The Godfather of Paparazzi

200 Jackie Onassis filed two lawsuits against him, Marlon Brando broke his jaw, Richard Burton's bodyguards beat him up, Elvis's bodyguards slashed his tires, and he was banned twice from Studio 54.

Ron Galella was America's original rogue photographer—the first to capture the stars off the red carpet. It was he who started the hunt for the never-before-seen photo. Without him, there would be no TMZ. So it comes as no surprise that *Vanity Fair* dubbed him "the Godfather of the U.S. paparazzi culture."

Galella started out as a photographer for the United States Air Force during the Korean War. He went on to study photojournalism in Los Angeles before moving to New York with his Rolleiflex camera in 1958. "I was forced to become a paparazzo to get out of poverty," he said.

Today, his impressive neoclassical home, flanked by white columns, marble rabbits and a fountain, is straight out of an episode of *The Sopranos*. At the base of the stairs, Galella's handprints are cast in the concrete—his own personal Hollywood Walk of Fame. The walls of his immense atrium are covered with black and white photographs of his famous subjects, featuring Lennon, Taylor, Kennedy, Warhol, Newman and Jagger, to name a few.

"My idea of a good picture is one that's in focus and of a famous person doing something unfamous," Andy Warhol famously said—and Galella made a fortune doing just that. "We had a lot in common. Like me, Andy did not want to miss anything. We went out every night. He said I was his favorite photographer. He would have liked to do what I did, but he was too shy," Galella explained, while his wife Betty watched TV in the kitchen. They have been living together for 35 years, and she negotiates the photo sales.

The choicest spot above the fireplace is reserved for his most iconic photo. "I call it *Windblown Jackie*. She has a Mona Lisa smile," Galella told me. The photo shows Jackie Onassis crossing Madison Avenue, windswept hair obscuring her face and enigmatic smile. That photo alone is said to have earned him a million dollars.

The photo was shot from a taxi. "That's probably why she was smiling. She didn't know it was me," explained Galella, who had a rather sordid relationship with his muse, Jacqueline Kennedy. "She was my favorite subject. She turned me into a paparazzo because she would never pose for photos."

He went to great lengths to pursue Jackie, hiding behind a restaurant coat rack, and even in the bushes to catch her bike riding through Central Park with her kids. She once ordered her bodyguard to "smash his camera," and took him to court twice. The 1972 trial lasted 26 days and resulted in a restraining order to keep Galella 7.5 meters (25 feet) from the Kennedys. To this day, he is banned from photographing Caroline Kennedy. Despite all this, he believes that Jackie enjoyed the game. "She was a hypocrite. I think she liked being chased. I've been told that she had a copy of my book of Jackie photographs in her library."

Jackie wasn't the only star Galella tangled with. "Sinatra once called me a Wop." And Galella and Marlon Brando had a longstanding feud. One night in Chinatown, in June of 1973, fed up with being followed, Brando motioned for the photographer to come closer. "He asked what I wanted. I told him I wanted to take a picture of him without glasses, and that's when he punched me. I lost five teeth," Galella explained, laughing. The lawsuit was settled out of court, and Galella came away with $40,000 in his pocket.

When he tried to get a shot of the actor a year later, Galella showed up wearing a football helmet. The photo was seen around the world, and became an ongoing gag with celebrities, who would pretend to punch the paparazzo in the head.

The man who once spent a weekend camped out in a rat-infested factory to get a shot of Liz Taylor and Richard Burton on their yacht no longer has quite the same verve as he did in his early days. But while old age and bad knees keep him from running the red carpet, he can still be seen with his trusty camera draped around his neck.

He has four employees who manage his basement archives, which contain three million photos of celebrities in hundreds of boxes piled from floor to ceiling. Newman, Sinatra, Travolta and Minnelli have an entire room to themselves.

"It was easier back then. There weren't as many bodyguards and PR people to get in the way of the work. Nowadays it's too crowded—there are too many photographers and it's dangerous."

Galella still enjoys developing his own photos and has turned his attention to publishing books. As he contemplates the archives, he looks back with nostalgia on those golden years: "It was the golden age of glamor. All the best photos are already in my archives." For Galella, the hunt is over.

New York's Green Lung

201

Central Park is New York's greatest treasure. The 3.4-square-kilometer (1.3-square-mile) park was designed in 1857 by landscape architect Frederick Law Olmsted. During the summer, I love getting a group of friends together, grabbing some food and heading out for a picnic in the grass by Turtle Pond, the home of huge turtles. With the **Belvedere Castle** (A) in the background, it feels like being in a movie. The neo-Gothic castle, which they started to build in 1869, was originally designed as a point of reference for the park's visitors. Since 1919, the American National Weather Service has been gathering all kinds of data there, such as temperature, rainfall and wind direction. The castle is located at 79th Street.

In the summer, I love sitting on the terrace at the restaurant **Le Pain Quotidien**—right by Sheep's Meadow—to watch people spread out on multi-colored blankets on the lawn. I take these opportunities to walk down the zoo's central path just to see the seal basin.

Right in the middle of the park, close to the Shakespeare garden, there's a puppet theater in an old Swedish cabin built in 1875. In the summertime, they put on daily kids shows. The theater is located at 79th Street and West Drive.

The cherry blossoms bloom in Central Park in April and May, making for a gorgeous display. The best spot to see them is on East Drive, right by the Metropolitan Museum of Art.

To feel a jolt of pure New York energy, I stop to watch the **Central Park Dance Skaters** (B), a roller-skating dance association. They've been getting together every weekend from April to October since the 1970s. Most of their participants are very eccentric. One of them often skates while balancing a water bottle on their head. Enter at 72nd Street and walk toward the middle of the park where you'll hear house music; they're easy to find.

The **Conservatory Garden** (C) is Central Park's only gated garden. You can access it from 5th Avenue at 105th Street, and it feels like discovering a privileged spot. First, you have to go through Vanderbilt Gate, the wrought-iron gate named after one of Manhattan's richest families (Anderson Cooper's family on his mother's side). It was the old entrance to the Vanderbilt estate in the 1930s. The garden is divided into three areas with French, Italian and English styles. Many weddings have been held there.

Take this opportunity to visit the **Museum of the City of New York** on the other side of 5th Avenue, outside of Central Park. They showcase exhibits on New York's history, culture and architecture. This is one of the museums that will teach you the most about the city [1220 5th Ave].

201C

201A

201B

Catching an Exhibit in an Old Armory

202

The **Park Avenue Armory**—headquarters of the National Guard's 7th Regiment during the Civil War—is one of the most impressive cultural spaces in town. Nowadays, they put on plays, concerts and immersive audio-visual installations. The space—reminiscent of a European train station—has an area of over 5,000 square meters (54,000 square feet). If you want to check the schedule, visit their website at armoryonpark.org [643 Park Ave].

The Mayor of Strawberry Fields

203

Gary Dos Santos was an odd duck. For about 20 years, this homeless man was sort of the guardian of Strawberry Fields: John Lennon's memorial located just a few steps away from the Dakota Building where the famous Beatle was murdered on December 8, 1980, and where Yoko Ono still lives. Each year, on the anniversary of Lennon's death, she lights a candle at 11:15 p.m. at the 7th floor's first window.

After Lennon's death, Gary Dos Santos started going to Strawberry Fields and leaving flowers, cherries and strawberries—given to him by grocers—on the *Imagine* mosaic. I was once fortunate enough to interview Dos Santos. While pointing toward the park bench where he spent his days with his black lab Mary Jane, he told me: "A few years ago, Lennon came to see me in a dream and told me to continue what I was doing, so I come here every day. I was sick of those dumb guides telling tourists whatever they felt like." He therefore proclaimed himself guardian of the grounds and talked about Lennon to whoever would lend him an ear. In 2009, director Torre Catalano made a documentary about Dos Santos, *The Mayor of Strawberry Fields*. Gary even met Yoko Ono.

Every December 8, thousands of people gather there to pay tribute to John Lennon, and Gary Dos Santos arranged this huge hippy mass for years. "The number of people varies from year to year," he explained to me, "it all depends on the weather." Gary referred to Lennon as his "brother." He died of leukemia in 2013.

A Milk Shake Circa 1940

204 **Lexington Candy Shop** reminds me of Lou's Cafe from *Back to the Future*. The luncheonette is a beloved neighborhood institution that's been open since 1925. This place hasn't been renovated since 1948, and they still serve the same classic American dishes (milk shakes, lemonade, sodas, sundaes and burgers). Even the milk shake blender is from the 1940s. The restaurant that's appeared in many films has belonged to the same family for three generations. Don't miss their collection of old Coca-Cola bottles on display in the window [1226 Lexington Ave].

The Open-Air Gallery

205 In East Harlem, the court at the Jackie Robinson Educational Complex is nicknamed the "***Graffiti Hall of Fame***." The school has allowed local and international taggers to paint graffiti on its exterior walls since the 1980s. Over the years, this place has become a true street art gallery (E 106th St and Park Ave).

Over two kilometers (1.2 miles) north, at a sports court at the corner of 2nd Avenue and East 128th Street, you'll see Keith Haring's famous orange mural, ***Crack is Wack***. It was completed in 1986 and restored in 2007.

Celebrate Museums

206

The **Museum Mile** festival has taken place each June since 1978. It's named after the stretch of 5th Avenue between 82nd and 105th streets where there are almost a dozen museums. Admission to the nine museums is free for the festival, 5th Avenue is closed to car traffic, musicians take over, and kids draw on the pavement with colored chalk. Check festival dates on the website museummilefestival.org.

Here are the five must-see museums:

1- The **Metropolitan Museum of Art** (A) is New York's largest and most prestigious museum. You could spend days there and not see everything. Don't miss the Anna Wintour Costume Center, Egyptian gallery, weapons and armor room (some are from 400 BC), and rooms dedicated to European and American painting where you can see pieces by Picasso, Matisse, Miró, Sargent, Homer, Whistler, etc. Few people know this, but the admission price ($25 for adults, $17 for seniors and $12 for students) is only a suggested guideline. You can actually pay what you like (or what you can). Don't forget to visit the rooftop garden where they show a different installation every summer. They have a martini bar on Fridays and Saturdays starting at 5:30 p.m. [1000 5th Ave].

2- The **Cooper Hewitt** museum is entirely devoted to contemporary design. It's located in the house of American industrialist Andrew Carnegie; he also commissioned the construction of the famous venue Carnegie Hall in 1891 [2 E 91st St].

3- Another museum located in the old house of a rich New York industrialist, **The Frick Collection** showcases work by European artists from before the 20th century. It's definitely worth a visit, if only to assess the opulence in which certain New Yorkers lived in the 19th century, including Henry Clay Frick. The construction of this small palace—including two magnificent bowling lanes in the basement, sadly closed to the public—lasted two years and cost $5 million (land included), a huge sum at the time. Mr. Frick actually only lived in the house for five years when he died of a heart attack in 1919. He wished for his house to become a museum after his and his spouse's death. Admission price is $20 ($15 for seniors and $10 for students), except from 11 a.m. to 1 p.m. on Sundays,

206 B

when contributions are left up to your discretion (1 E 70th St).

4- A Frank Lloyd Wright masterpiece, the **Guggenheim** (B) museum's unique architecture practically steals the show from its artwork, which was actually a point of criticism when the museum opened in 1959. They say that its helical structure is a headache for exhibit curators. The best way to visit this place is to start at the top of the spiral and go downward, in accordance with Mr. Wright's wishes. On Saturdays from 5:45 p.m. to 7:45 p.m., admission is at your discretion, but not free. On those days, the last visitors are let in at 7:15 p.m. [1071 5th Ave].

5- Established in a mansion built in 1914 that was inhabited by many members of New Yorker's upper class (including the Vanderbilts), the **Neue Galerie** (C) is a museum of early 20th-century German and Austrian art. The museum's restaurant, **Café Sabarsky**, is a must. Inspired by Vienna's great cafes, this establishment serves excellent apple strudel and often hosts classical music concerts. Admission is free from 6:00 p.m. to 8:00 p.m. on the first Friday of the month [1048 5th Ave].

Cocktails With a View

207 For a next-level drink with a view of Central Park, **The Roof**—the Viceroy hotel's rooftop bar— is one of the most gorgeous spots in town. The decor made entirely of wood reminds me of a luxurious yacht's interior. This place is open to the public from 4:00 p.m. to 4 a.m., but I recommend going at dusk to snap photos of buildings lighting up [124 W 57th St].

Claire's Closet

208 **Fivestory** is a luxury store that specializes in creations by independent designers. The five-story shop belongs to young New Yorker Claire Distenfeld. The clothing is quite expensive; I go mostly to browse the jewelry and shoe garden, and to discover the latest designers. Going there feels like visiting the boudoir of a rich friend who grew up on the Upper East Side. Unlike the shops on Madison Street, the staff here is welcoming and knows how to make you feel comfortable [18 E 69th St].

The Store With Absolutely Everything

209 A family business that set up shop in 1950, **Zitomer** is more than a simple drugstore. They sell everything: European cosmetics, rare perfume, house-brand products (Z New York), costumes, jewelry, diadems, wigs, high-end children's clothing, toys and even clothes for animals. This spot is as kitschy as you can imagine with its 1970s decor and neon signs. You'll feel transported to another era, and leave with products you didn't need in the first place! [969 Madison Ave].

Bill's Perspective

210 In New York, everyone wants to be photographed by **Bill Cunningham**, one of the first street fashion photographers in the United States. In the fashion industry, he is as iconic as the Empire State Building.

Each week, Bill puts his finger on the pulse of Manhattan in his *New York Times* columns "On the Street" and "Evening Hours." He is part of the newspaper's heart and soul, and spots new trends before anyone else.

Bill Cunningham's office is the street. He works day and night, rain or shine. With his trusty Nikon camera around his neck, wearing his usual blue coat, he jumps on his 29th Schwinn bicycle (the previous 28 were all stolen) and heads for the corner of 5th Avenue and 57th Street—his favorite spot to snap stylish New Yorkers.

Now in his eighties, Bill has never compromised on his art. He could have become rich, but instead made the rather radical decision not to accept money for his photographs. He believes that this is the best way to stay honest and independent. When he covers an event, he refuses to accept even a glass of water.

In 2010, filmmaker Richard Press made a documentary about him called *Bill Cunningham New York*. For the first time, it revealed details about the life of this enigmatic character, like his tiny apartment with no cupboards, no kitchen and no private bathroom.

Bill is content with very little and lives surrounded by filing cabinets and boxes of photographs stacked to the ceiling. At the time the documentary was released, Bill was still using film, and since the *New York Times* no longer had a photo lab, he was developing his photos in a 43rd Street shop. These days, Bill works with a digital camera.

Nothing can stop Bill Cunningham—not even old age. I'll never forget the night I saw him bicycling up 6th Avenue in a snowstorm, with only a single plastic bag protecting him. Here is someone who truly understands that in New York, the show is on the street.

People here talk about money without shame. A person on the subway might just very well ask you how much you pay for rent. Don't worry, it is completely normal; New Yorkers are obsessed with real estate. #onlyinNY

The Upper East Side's Restaurants

211

The East Pole is a restaurant located in a brownstone (the famous red sandstone New York buildings). The walls are covered with old maps, and there's a lovely terrace in the back. Must-tries: the tomato soup with a grilled cheese, truffle and Parmesan chips, and the fennel-tarragon-lobster fish pie [133 E 65th St].

To mingle with the Upper East Side's bourgeoisie or catch a glimpse of celebrities or designers, **Sant Ambroeus**—a chic Milanese restaurant—is the place to be. There's a cafe area with a gelato counter at the front, and they prepare delicious panini to go [1000 Madison Ave].

For a snack after touring the museums, I recommend **Yura on Madison**: a delicatessen that serves takeout meals, sandwiches, salads and coffee. Take a seat by the window or on one of the outdoor benches, and watch the Upper East Side wildlife in action [1292 Madison Ave].

After a visit to the Metropolitan Museum of Art, I often stop in at **Via Quadronno**, an adorable Milanese cafe patronized by local regulars and a few Italian tourists. They serve panini at the front. For a full meal, sit in the dining room at the back [25 E 73rd St].

Fashion lovers should add Freds restaurant (on the 9th floor of the huge department store, **Barneys**) to their list. Many magazine editors eat there between meetings [660 Madison Ave].

Cafe Mingala is the only Burmese restaurant in New York, and is a well-kept neighborhood secret. It might not look like much, but the food is absolutely delicious. A three-course lunch barely costs $7. Try the fermented tea-leaf salad [1393 B 2nd Ave].

Orsay, a French restaurant reminiscent of Paris' great *brasseries* with its art nouveau style, is my destination of choice for a long weekend meal with friends. They have a fixed-price brunch menu that includes pastries, an appetizer and main course ($29.50). Try the cheese soufflé or salmon tartar [1057 Lexington Ave].

Andy Warhol's Muse

212

Susan Blond was Andy Warhol's muse in the 1970s, and is one of the most famous publicits in New York. She shared the Studio 54 dance floor with Michael Jackson in the *Thriller* era, and was a good friend of James Brown. Spending two hours with her was like diving into the heart of the intellectual and hip New York of the 1970s and 1980s.

The walls of her chic Midtown office are decorated with paintings given to her by Keith Haring, Andy Warhol and Jean-Michel Basquiat. The decor is rounded out by signed posters of Mick Jagger and Patti Smith, and a photo of Susan in her first Chanel suit for *Vogue* magazine. "The miracle is that it still fits me," she says, with a burst of laughter. "James Brown and Michael Jackson loved that outfit."

Born in New York to a Jewish family, Susan Blond studied music, and then painting, at a Harlem arts school. Her classmates included people like Julian Schnabel who went on to become renowned artists.

In the late 1960s, she became part of Andy Warhol's Factory and inner circle. "The first time I met Andy he said to me: "Susan Blond... I love your name, I love your voice, I'm going to put you in all of my films!" And that's how she became one of his muses. "My most memorable role was the woman who throws the baby out the window in *Bad*, the last film that Andy produced."

Susan says that Warhol would love today's world, where people are constantly taking photos on their phone, tweeting and blogging. "He was the first to film and

photograph everything," she explained. Today, Warhol's famous quote "In the future, everyone will be famous for fifteen minutes," seems rather prophetic.

It was thanks to Warhol that Susan became a publicist, since she was part of the team when he founded *Interview* magazine. "Going out with Andy was fabulous," she reminisced. "Everyone felt like a star when they were near him. Everyone loved him, even the cops. When we went to shows at Madison Square Garden, they cleared the streets so we could go."

At the Factory, Susan rubbed shoulders with the likes of Paloma Picasso, Mick Jagger and Dennis Hopper, among others. "The seventies was a crazy time. But I didn't take drugs. I was already enough of an extrovert—and Andy hated drugs."

She remembers Andy Warhol as a highly disciplined man who was more traditional than you might think. He preferred brunettes to bleach blonds, and Burberry coats to leather jackets. "He came to work even on Saturdays and he went to church regularly. He chose the smallest office in the Factory."

In the 1980s, Susan became the first female vice president at Epic Records, where she worked with Tina Turner, Prince, Boy George, James Brown and Iggy Pop. "We were making huge amounts of money, and it was the golden age of the record industry. We threw fabulous parties."

And what about Michael Jackson? "I would take him to Studio 54 and Chez Régine, and I'd say to him, "Come and dance, Michael," and he would say, "No, dancing is work." He was such a perfectionist!" Susan was partly responsible for the success of *Thriller*, one of the most popular albums of all time.

Did she know from the start that it would be such a huge success? "Oh yes, instantly!"

There is a sense of sadness when she talks about Michael Jackson. "I loved him. He was childlike, but also the most sophisticated person I've ever known. He knew what he wanted. I'm glad I didn't have to represent him toward the end of his life, when everything was going wrong."

The Bobo Neighborhood With Sumptuous Houses

Upper West Side

Upper West Side

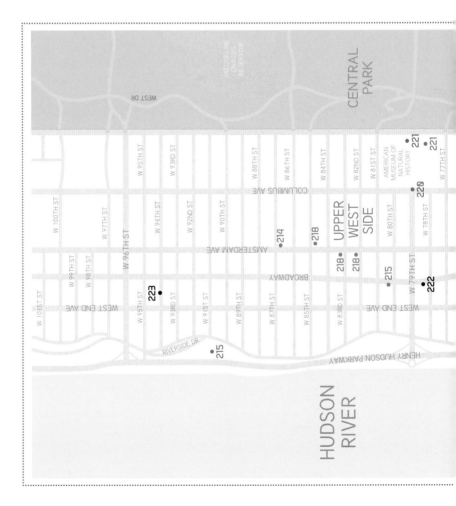

CENTRAL PARK

JACQUELINE ONASSIS RESERVOIR

WEST DR

W 100TH ST
W 95TH ST
W 93RD ST
W 85TH ST
W 86TH ST
W 84TH ST
W 82ND ST
W 81ST ST
AMERICAN MUSEUM OF NATURAL HISTORY
W 77TH ST

221
221

COLUMBUS AVE

W 97TH ST
W 96TH ST
W 94TH ST
W 92ND ST
W 90TH ST
W 80TH ST
W 78TH ST

220

214

218

UPPER WEST SIDE

AMSTERDAM AVE

W 99TH ST
W 98TH ST
W 79TH ST

218
218

215

BROADWAY

223

222

W 101ST ST
W 95TH ST
W 93RD ST
W 91ST ST
W 89TH ST
W 87TH ST
W 85TH ST
W 83RD ST

WEST END AVE
WEST END AVE

RIVERSIDE DR

215

HENRY HUDSON PARKWAY

HUDSON RIVER

The Bobo Neighborhood With Sumptuous Houses

Sights + photo ops
Bars + restaurants
Stores + markets
Arts + culture
Activities + walks

Levain Bakery

213

BARNEY GREENGRASS THE Sturgeon KING

THE STURGEON KING

214

Pam and Connie's Cookies

213

Levain Bakery is a small bakery that specializes in cookies. Friends Connie McDonald and Pam Weekes founded this business in 1994 after leaving behind their careers (in finance and fashion respectively) to bake the best cookies in New York. Try their chocolate chip and nut treats; they're huge and weigh in at almost 170 grams (six ounces). The two bakers also make excellent raisin buns, but only on the weekend. I love taking a seat on the bench in front of the bakery to watch the everyday lives of the neighborhood's residents [167 W 74th St].

The King of Smoked Fish

214

If you're visiting the Upper West Side, set out toward **Barney Greengrass**. This spot is one of the rare family institutions still alive and well in Manhattan, much like Katz's Delicatessen or Russ and Daughters. The deli—a restaurant and appetizing store—has belonged to the Greengrass family for over 105 years. Don't miss out on the smoked sturgeon sandwich with cream cheese, onions and tomatoes on Bialy bread (a kind of lighter onion bagel without a hole, a bit like an English muffin). In the restaurant section, you can dine on scrambled eggs with smoked salmon. I love this place for its decor that seems frozen in time. They actually filmed many scenes here for the movie *Extremely Loud and Incredibly Close*, featuring Tom Hanks and Sandra Bullock [541 Amsterdam Ave].

215

The Unknown Garden

215

For a romantic date (modeled on Tom Hanks and Meg Ryan in *You've Got Mail*), I recommend **Community Garden**: a garden unfamiliar to tourists at 91st Street in Riverside Park. If you want to have a picnic, stock up on bagels, smoked fish, olives and cheese at local institution Zabar's [2245 Broadway].

The Man Who Draws New York

216

For over 50 years, New York has been **Bruce McCall**'s muse. The Canadian-born artist is one of the most famous illustrators in the United States and a celebrity in the New York media world. Since 1979, he has been creating retrofuturist covers for *The New Yorker* and drawings for *Vanity Fair*.

I have admired McCall's work for a long time. I met him at Café Luxembourg—his second office, not far from his home in the Upper West Side. The hostess always reserves him the same seat. This is where he used to eat with his friend, the writer Mordecai Richler. He still comes here to meet his friends—like actor Steve Martin, who usually arrives on bicycle.

McCall left Toronto in the 1960s. After a brief stay in Detroit, he joined the New York advertising world, which he describes as exactly like the one portrayed on *Mad Men*.

"I'll never forget my second day at the office. My bosses invited me to lunch and ordered three rounds of Manhattans (a cocktail made from whiskey, vermouth and bitters). It was normal at the time, and we kept it up for the next five years. We would get back to the office at three in the afternoon, nap for two hours, and then go home."

Twenty-five years later, Bruce left advertising to become an illustrator. His first opportunity came from the *National Lampoon* humor magazine.

In 1979, he finally found the courage to contact *The New Yorker*. "I was scared because I've always suffered from

217

imposter syndrome. I never finished high school, I'm not an intellectual, and I'm a foreigner. Instead, they said "Where have you been all these years?" It just goes to show that in New York, you have to be willing to take a chance. "Even after all these years, I'm still an outsider—and that's what allows me to take a fresh look at the city and see the absurdity of everyday life."

McCall's style is unique. "I've been doing the same thing since I was eight years old. My style hasn't changed very much. It's all I know how to do." He still uses gouache.

His highly imaginative imagery is influenced by 1950s magazines and their absurd and surreal advertisements, which depicted flying cars, blimps, tunnels to China and miracle drugs. "It was also my way of escaping throughout my childhood. I immersed myself in those magazines to forget about my family life—my alcoholic mother and tyrannical father."

Since then, McCall has developed his own vocabulary to describe his illustrations, using terms like "faux nostalgia," "hyperbolic exaggeration," "urban absurdism," and "techno-archeology."

The man who draws his inspiration from our obsession with progress refers to himself as a "dinosaur." He doesn't have a cell phone and, he elaborates, "I don't even know the difference between a PC and a Mac."

Five-Star Brunch in the Clouds

217 Brunch at **Asiate** in the Mandarin Oriental hotel is a unique experience. Located on the 35th floor with a breathtaking view of Central Park through bay windows, this is a restaurant for special occasions. The tasting brunch costs $64; if you're looking to impress or treat someone, this is where you want to reserve a table. At the end of the meal, you're welcome to fill up a small box with chocolates as a souvenir from your visit [80 Columbus Circle].

The Bobo Restaurants

218

Before catching a show at Lincoln Center or a musical on Broadway, I usually grab a bite to eat at **Blue Ribbon Sushi Bar & Grill**, a cozy, little-known spot hidden in the 6 Columbus hotel. Try their spicy crab and shiso leaf rolls, and the Hamachi Tataki appetizer: a fish tartar with quail eggs [308 W 58th St].

Another pre-show possibility is **Boulud Sud**, one of many New York restaurants— this one Mediterranean-inspired— by French chef Daniel Boulud. The $60 pre-theater, fixed-price menu includes an appetizer, main course and dessert (20 W 64th St).

On the other side of the street at the Lincoln Center plaza, the green roof above **Hypar Pavilion** (A) is worth the trip. You can access it from West 65th Street just west of Broadway.

Charcuterie lovers will want to try **Salumeria Rosi Parmacotto**, an Upper West Side standard. This small 32-seat Italian restaurant is one of chef Anthony Bourdain's favorites. Chef Cesare Casella brings Parma ham (*prosciutto di Parma*) back from his trips to Emilia-Romagna. Order their salami and cheese platter, along with the lasagna [283 Amsterdam Ave].

At **Cafe Lalo** (B), where desserts are the specialty, they sell 100 kinds of pies, cakes and pastries. I like the lively atmosphere of this spot with a pseudo-European decor. Brunch is served until 4 p.m. and costs between $5 and $20. I like heading over late at night after leaving the movies or theater. The restaurant closes at two in the morning, but at 4 a.m. on Friday and Saturday [201 W 83rd St].

For a healthier option, **Peacefood Cafe** right next door serves excellent vegan desserts and smoothies [460 Amsterdam Ave].

218A

218B

To pickle, craft beer and comfort food lovers, I recommend **Jacob's Pickles**, a restaurant inspired by the culinary traditions of the American south. Owner Jacob Hadjigeorgis is known for his fried chicken sandwich on a biscuit. Everything is homemade at Jacob's, from the pickles to the jam. He prepares eight kinds of brined, pickled vegetables that can be purchased on the spot. It's an all-around popular eatery, whether it's during the day for brunch or at night for their wide selection of cocktails (try the Bloody B.L.T.) and 26 types of American craft beer [509 Amsterdam Ave].

Jazz With a View of Central Park

219 **Jazz at Lincoln Center** is one of my favorite concert venues, and by far the one with the most beautiful view. They put on many concerts per week, from tributes to George Gershwin to concerts by students of the prestigious Julliard School. The complex entirely dedicated to jazz music has three rooms (Rose Theatre, Appel Room and Dizzy's Club) that overlook Columbus Circle and Central Park. The entrance is in the Time Warner Center [33 W 60th St]. You can buy tickets from this website: jazzatlincolncenter.org.

Dancing at the Planetarium

220 Next to the museum, beneath a huge glass cube, you'll find the **Rose Center for Earth and Space**. The planetarium shows a 3-D movie about the Big Bang and the cosmos. If you've seen Woody Allen's *Manhattan*, you'll recognize the setting: Isaac and Mary find shelter there during a storm. Since 2007, the museum has hosted the popular One Step Beyond parties with different DJs in the Hall of Planet Earth. You can buy tickets ahead of time (amnh.org/tickets) or at the door [Weston Pavilion, Columbus Ave and 79th St].

Get into a taxi and then tell the driver your destination. Never do it the other way around or the cab could slip through your fingers. New York taxi drivers aren't allowed to choose customers based on their destination, but it can still happen. #onlyinNY

A Night at the Museum

221 The **American Museum of Natural History** is probably the only museum in New York that's as interesting for kids as for adults. The museum is especially famous for its life-sized, suspended blue whale in the Hall of Ocean Life. Their collections bring together over 30 million specimens (insects, fossils, mammals and precious stones). Don't miss the Star of India in the Hall of Gems. The 563-carat blue sapphire is two billion years old. They suggest $22 a ticket, but payment is left up to your discretion [Central Park W and 79th].

An activity that needs to be planned in advance is the sleepover for kids six to 13 years old (accompanied by at least one parent). The event that takes place twice a month in the summer is inspired by the movie *Night at the Museum*. After a series of museum activities, the kids go to bed in sleeping bags beneath the blue whale or in the Hall of Dinosaurs. A snack is served in the evening, along with breakfast the next morning. You can easily reserve by phone (212-769-5200), and tickets cost $145 per person.

When New York Looks Like Paris and Florence

222

Many residential buildings in the Upper West Side are reminiscent of Paris' Haussmannian architecture. Take the **Ansonia** (A) [2109 Broadway] for example, an old hotel residence converted into condos in 1992, originally designed by French architect Paul-Émile Duboy. Built between 1899 and 1904, it was the first New York hotel to have air conditioning. Many famous people stayed there, including New York Yankee great Babe Ruth. Musicians like Stravinsky were attracted by the thickness of its walls. There was once a farm on the roof where many animals lived, including chickens, ducks and even a tamed bear. An employee delivered fresh eggs to each tenant every morning. It's one of those buildings that will make you dream of a bygone New York.

The **Apple Bank** across the way [2100 Broadway] was built in 1926. Go in to gaze at the 20-meter (65½-foot) high ceilings and architecture inspired by a Florentine palace.

The Apthorp [2211 Broadway] (B) is a historical residential building modeled on Florence's Palazzo Pitti. Scriptwriter Nora Ephron lived there for 10 years, as did stars like Cyndi Lauper and Al Pacino. Sadly, the building has lost some of its soul in the last few years due to numerous renovations. The residential complex takes up an entire block, and was inaugurated by the Astor family in 1908. It's been the backdrop of many movies, including Francis Ford Coppola's *The Cotton Club*. Ask the guard for permission to see the courtyard; it's a unique place.

222A

223

A Village in the Middle of the City

222B

223 I still remember the thrill I felt upon discovering this hidden gem right in the heart of Manhattan. **Pomander Walk** is an English-style pedestrian walkway located between W 94th and W 95th streets, west of Broadway. The 16-house, Tudor-style complex dates back to 1922. Many families still live there today, as if on a movie set. The houses with decorative shutters are painted red, green or blue, and they all have a miniature garden. I was able to visit the grounds after waiting patiently in front of the iron gates. At a certain point, a resident let me in so that I could take photos. Some do open the gate for curious onlookers; just be patient. This place was threatened with destruction for a long time due to the property value, but Pomander Walk was registered as a historic monument in 1982.

Comfort Food Set to Jazz

Morningside Heights, Harlem, Inwood

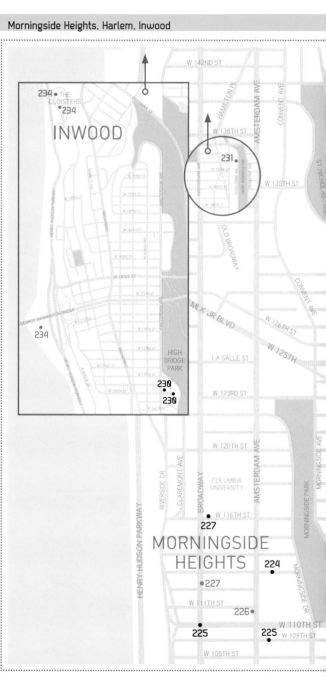

INWOOD

234 THE CLOISTERS
234

231

234

230
230

227

MORNINGSIDE HEIGHTS

224

227

226

225   225

Sights + photo ops
Bars + restaurants
Stores + markets
Arts + culture
Activities + walks

The Unfinished Cathedral

224

Much like Barcelona's Sagrada Família, New York has its own cathedral that's still unfinished 120 years after construction began. **Saint John the Divine** is the seat of New York's diocese, one of the 100 dioceses of the United States' Episcopal Church. The work began in 1892, but has been stopped for over 20 years.

They say that Saint John the Divine is the largest cathedral in the world. It's so tall that the Statue of Liberty (without its pedestal) could fit standing up beneath the central dome, and is long enough to hold two football fields.

The cathedral has also been used as an exhibition and creative space for artists-in-residence since the 1970s. One of them was Philippe Petit, the famous French tightrope walker who crossed the distance between the two World Trade Center towers on an iron wire in 1974 (see reason No. 3). You can see a Keith Haring sculpture—*The Life of Christ*—in the chapel: his only religious piece made a few months before his death.

The gardens surrounding the cathedral are home to three free-ranging peacocks: Jim, Harry and Phil. The latter is albino and has his own Twitter account (@CathedralPhil). The church also has a beehive and makes its own honey: Divine Honey.

In the spring, cyclists come to have their bikes blessed before the summer season (theblessingofthebikes.com). A parishioner suggested this idea over 15 years ago. During the brief ceremony, hundreds of cyclists in bike shorts go into the cathedral with their bikes, which the reverend then sprays with holy water; a truly surprising sight [1047 Amsterdam Ave].

Obama's Start in New York

225

Broadway at the corner of West 110th Street is where **Barack Obama** got off the subway with his suitcase in hand on an August evening in 1981. He was 20 years old and arriving from Los Angeles to study at Columbia University. His first night is worthy of a Scorsese *After Hours*-style film. When he got to the door of the building he was supposed to live in [142 W 109th St], no one was there. Since he had no money to pay for a hotel room, he decided to spend the night in a nearby alleyway. The next day, he washed using water from a fire hydrant, next to a homeless person. It's a rather romantic image, especially when you consider what was in store for him.

We know very little about Obama's four years in New York. He isn't very talkative about this chapter of his life, and he only scratches the surface of it in his autobiography *Dreams from My Father*. However, these years were crucial for him, as they are when he became a political activist. "He wanted to be a writer back then," remembers his old roommate, Phil Boerner.

Their apartment was very far from offering the comforts of the White House. "The doorbell didn't work and there had been a fire in the apartment across the hall. It was very cramped, there was no shower, only a bathtub, and no doors to the bedrooms," recounts Boerner who now lives in California. "Heating was intermittent, so we had to study in sleeping bags. Since we rarely had hot water, we showered at Columbia University's gym." Rent cost $360 a month back then, the equivalent of $2,000 today.

227 B

The Writers' Cafe

26 Since the 1950s, **Hungarian Pastry Shop** has been a favorite cafe with Morningside Heights' writers and Columbia University students. Order a cappuccino and cherry strudel, and sit down at a table with a good book. It's one of the few Wi-Fi-free cafes left, which is a big part of its charm [1030 Amsterdam Ave].

The Seinfeld Diner

227 **Tom's Restaurant** (A) has been a Morningside Heights institution since the 1940s. The family business became famous in the 1990s thanks to the TV show *Seinfeld*: You can see their red, neon sign in almost every episode. The interior scenes, however, were filmed in a studio. Jerry Seinfeld, who lives in the Upper West Side, still drops in from time to time. That's also where Barack Obama had breakfast before his classes at Columbia in the 1980s.

Nowadays, you can chat with old philosophy professors sitting at the counter with a cup of coffee during the day. At night, college students take over this spot for milk shakes and fries [2880 Broadway].

While you're in the area, you might as well check out the **Columbia campus** (B). Founded in 1754, it's the oldest university in the State of New York. You'll find one of the entrances on Broadway at the corner of West 116th Street.

227 A

228A 229

Gospel Service

228 It's Sunday morning in New York and you're looking for a unique experience. Hop on the subway, head to Harlem and attend a gospel church service. Here are a few places where tourists are more than welcome:

1- **Mother African Methodist Episcopal Zion Church** (A) has a religious service that begins at 11 a.m. [140 W 137th St].
2- **Abyssinian Baptist Church** has one of the best choirs. Get there around 9:30 a.m. if you want a seat; pews fill up fast [132 W 138th St].
3- The small **New Mount Zion Baptist Church** has been one of the most popular churches for over 80 years. It's full of energy and there's music throughout the service [171 W 140th St].
4- The **Mount Neboh Baptist Church** choir is a local favorite for their rendition of *Oh Happy Day* [1883 7th Ave].

If you don't want to wait in line or don't feel up to going into these churches, Harlem Heritage organizes guided tours of the neighborhood and its gospel churches (harlemheritage.com).

The Restaurant Where the Music Never Stops

229 Red Rooster—chef Marcus Samuelsson's restaurant—has been a popular destination since it opened at the end of 2010, drawing the downtown crowd all the way to Harlem. The clientele at Red Rooster is the most diverse I've seen in New York. The live venue in the basement transforms into a dance floor at around 10 p.m. with house and hip-hop DJ contests. The Sunday brunch with gospel music is very popular. Try the Caesar salad, corn bread, Dirty Rice & Shrimp, Mac & Greens and Oxtail Pappardelle. The fastest way to get there is by subway on the 2 or 3 lines. The restaurant is right next to the 125th Street station's exit [310 Lenox Ave].

230

231

The Oldest House in New York

230

A few blocks away from Marjorie's (see reason No. 231), you'll find Manhattan's oldest residence, the **Morris-Jumel Mansion**. The large white house with Palladian columns was built in 1765, and George Washington stayed there in 1776 during the Revolutionary War. The City of New York bought the house in 1903 and established a museum devoted to the revolutionary era that's filled with period furniture [65 Jumel Ter].

Even more amazing is the narrow, paved road facing the residence. Sylvan Terrace is lined with 20 wooden two-story houses that were featured in the first season of *Boardwalk Empire*. They were built in 1882 and used to be home to middle class families. Still in perfect condition, the houses now sell for nearly $1 million each. A staircase connects this cul-de-sac to Saint Nicholas Avenue, a bit north of West 160th Street. The 163rd Street subway stop on the C line is just steps away.

A Sunday Afternoon at Marjorie's

231

Marjorie Eliot has opened her apartment doors to strangers who want to hear some jazz from 4 p.m. to 6 p.m. every Sunday for the last 20 odd years. She pushes the furniture to the side and places chairs with cushions in her living room, kitchen and hallway. She lights scented candles, prepares cookie platters and serves glasses of juice.

At around 3:30 p.m., the first guests arrive at the door of apartment 3-F where the walls are covered with photos of Martin Luther King and Barack Obama. The audience is eclectic: old neighborhood friends, students and a few tourists.

The show begins at 4 p.m. on the nose. It features Bob Cunningham—an old jazz wolf on the upright bass—and Sedric Shukroon on the saxophone, while Marjorie's son Rudel Drears sings. Marjorie herself sits down at the piano in front of a picture of her son Philip who died of kidney failure on a Sunday in 1992.

This free concert that she puts on for the public 52 Sundays out of the year aims to celebrate Phil's memory, as well as that of her other son Michael who died of meningitis in 2006. In February 2011, her son Shaun, who suffers from mental illness, disappeared. He was found 33 days later in a Harlem hospital.

"This is the way I've found to turn my sadness into a happy experience," says Marjorie. The woman is a force of nature. There's a donation jar at the exit [555 Edgecombe Ave, apartment 3-F; the subway's C line to the 163rd Street station].

232A 232C   232B

Comfort Food

232
The menu at restaurant **The Cecil** (A) is a mix of Asian, American southern and Caribbean cuisines. Go on Saturday between 2 p.m. and 6 p.m. for their DJ Brunch set to the rhythms and sounds of world music, soul and jazz. Cocktails cost $14, and the menu is eclectic. Try waffles with duck confit, lobster salad or macaroni and cheese [210 W 118th St].

Next door, you'll find **Minton's** (B), the chic legendary jazz club from the 1930s that was recently converted into a restaurant. Musicians play each night during dinner. After 11:00 p.m., the place transforms into a nightclub. Cover at the bar is $10 from Thursday to Sunday ($15 on Wednesday) or $20 at a table ($25 on Wednesday). Note that there's a dress code [206 W 118th St].

For a retro 1950s diner experience, **Harlem Shake** (C) is your destination. Hamburgers, fried chicken sandwiches and milk shakes are the menu's stars, but there's also a kids' menu and vegan options. You can have a seat on the big terrace [100 W 124th St].

Sylvia Woods was the Harlem queen of soul food ever since she opened her restaurant **Sylvia's** (D) in 1962. When she died in 2012 at the age of 86, the neighborhood went into mourning, and her name was up on the Apollo Theater's marquis for many days. Her restaurant is still just as popular nowadays and is patronized by many politicians looking to take the population's pulse. Barack Obama and Caroline Kennedy are regulars. It's better to go during the week; customers tend to wait outside by the dozens on weekends [328 Malcolm X Blvd].

Another comfort food institution is **Melba's**. Friendly owner Melba Wilson is best known for her fried chicken and waffles recipe [300 W 114th St].

Good local spot, **Vinateria**, doesn't serve soul food, but rather cuisine with Spanish and Italian influences. The menu changes on a daily basis, depending on what's at the market. This restaurant that belongs to a Harlem couple has a lovely terrace [2211 Frederick Douglass Blvd].

232D

The Studio Taxi

233

He would have liked to be an artist, but didn't have the knack for it—so now he encourages his customers to express their artistic side through drawing. A ride with **Fabio Peralta** is anything but dull: The man with 40 years of experience driving a New York cab has turned his back seat into an artist's studio. While most New York taxi drivers talk on the phone, weaving in and out of traffic with little regard for their passengers, Peralta cautiously avoids potholes and comes to a gentle stop. After all, who knows what kind of masterpiece his next passenger will create?

There are more than 13,000 yellow cabs in Manhattan, and Fabio claims to be the only one to keep mementos of his passengers. Five years ago, growing tired of his old routine, he came up with the simple and brilliant idea to get each of his passengers to make him a drawing. So far, he has nearly 8,000.

I spent a few hours with him, sitting in the front seat as he looked for customers in the streets of Midtown. I wanted to see what it was all about. At one point, a hurried man in a jacket and tie got in the cab, face buried in his phone. At the first red light, Fabio turned and handed him a drawing board and pen. "Would you draw something for me?" he asked in his thick Dominican accent. Most customers ask "What for?" before immersing themselves in the drawing process—a simple pleasure often reserved for children.

People rarely refuse. Most businessmen are surprised at first, but then drop their phones and set to work with a calm focus, leaving behind the stress of the day—at least for the short duration of the ride. Fabio has unwittingly invented a form of therapy in the middle of the urban jungle.

"I never know who will get in my cab, or what those people will become, but I keep a small trace of their visit." It turns out that New Yorkers are a talented bunch—some of the drawings are really good! Occasionally people prefer to write, and share their secrets on the page, but Fabio chooses not to read them because, as he says, "It's their business."

Medieval Art and Carnivorous Plants

234

The Cloisters, a small, lost paradise in northern Manhattan, belongs to the Metropolitan Museum of Art. The museum—the only one in North America entirely dedicated to medieval art and architecture—houses a collection of over 5,000 European pieces spread throughout five cloisters. Among the most famous, we should mention the group of seven tapestries, *The Hunt of the Unicorn*, made from 1495 to 1505.

The Cloisters are not reproductions of old buildings, but rather authentic sections of French and Spanish monasteries constructed between the 12th and 15th centuries. In the 1930s, they were dismantled into pieces and transported to New York by boat where they underwent an identical, stone-by-stone reconstruction. The Rockefeller family financed the costly operation, and the museum opened its doors in 1938. Even if medieval art isn't your cup of tea, the space's beauty makes the trip worthwhile. Twenty minutes away from Times Square, perched atop a hill in Fort Tryon Park overlooking the Hudson River, it suddenly feels like being in Spain...

The museum also has three gardens where you can see ancient plant species. The Bonnefont garden on the lower level has an impressive collection of 300 plants used in the Middle Ages including indoor plants, cooking herbs, as well as medicinal and magic-related ones, etc. They even have carnivorous plants. The museum's gardeners run the blog metmuseum.org/in-season.

They have a cafe, and you can picnic on the grounds. I recommend getting there by bike (45 minutes from Midtown); the ride along the river is stunning. Some people swim near 177th Street, while others fish. You can also get there by subway (A line to the Dyckman Street station). Tickets cost $25, but admission is actually left up to your discretion [99 Margaret Corbin Dr].

A Mosaic of Villages

Brooklyn

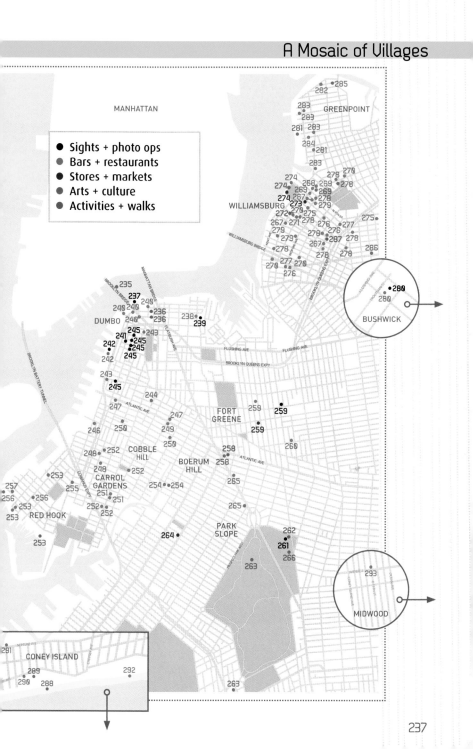

MANHATTAN

- Sights + photo ops
- Bars + restaurants
- Stores + markets
- Arts + culture
- Activities + walks

GREENPOINT

WILLIAMSBURG

WILLIAMSBURG BRIDGE

BROOKLYN QUEENS EXPY

BUSHWICK

BROOKLYN BRIDGE

MANHATTAN BRIDGE

DUMBO

FLATBUSH AVE

FLUSHING AVE

FLUSHING AVE

BROOKLYN QUEENS EXPY

BROOKLYN BATTERY TUNNEL

ATLANTIC AVE

FORT GREENE

COBBLE HILL

BOERUM HILL

ATLANTIC AVE

CARROL GARDENS

GOWANUS EXPY

RED HOOK

PARK SLOPE

MIDWOOD

CONEY ISLAND

New York's Most Beautiful Bridge

235

A stay in New York wouldn't be complete if you didn't cross the **Brooklyn Bridge** on foot: a New Yorker favorite. The best time to do it is at the end of the day, around sunset. It takes about 20 minutes to cross. Each day, 4,000 pedestrians and 3,100 cyclists use a level reserved exclusively for them. Here's a tip: if you don't want to upset New York cyclists, don't cross the white line that separates the two lanes.

Inaugurated in 1883, it's one of the oldest suspended bridges in the United States. Back then, there was a wine and champagne cellar in the abutment between the bridge's arches, on the Manhattan-facing side. You could get there by way of the Brooklyn Bridge–City Hall subway station. These spaces were rented out to absorb the astronomical costs of the bridge's construction, which was $15 million at the time. From 2010 to 2014, the bridge underwent large-scale renovations that cost half a billion dollars.

Art Under the Bridges

236

DUMBO (an acronym of the initials of Down Under the Manhattan Bridge Overpass) is mainly the Brooklyn art gallery district. Front, Water and Washington streets are packed with independent shops and cafes. I really like the **Powerhouse Arena** bookstore and art gallery [37 Main St]. On the second floor of **111 Front Street**, you'll come across a dozen galleries open to the public.

For a postcard-worthy photo of the Empire State Building between the Manhattan Bridge's feet, stand at the corner of Front and Washington streets.

The best way to get to DUMBO is to take the A or C subway trains [High Street–Brooklyn Bridge station] or cross the Brooklyn Bridge on foot. Go down the stairs on the left at the end of the pedestrian and cyclist lanes, and you're there.

235

The Carousel in a Glass Cube

237 At **Brooklyn Bridge Park** by the East River, there's an old carousel from the 1920s, the Jane Carousel. Kids are crazy about it. A huge glass cube designed by French architect Jean Nouvel protects the ride. The view of the Brooklyn Bridge from there is amazing [1 Water St]. There are often art exhibits in this park and food markets at Pier 5 on weekends. You'll find about 100 different kiosks.

A Neighborhood Frozen in Time

238

Vinegar Hill is a small neighborhood east of DUMBO with paved streets where time seems to have stopped. Hudson Avenue at Water Street is lined with houses built before the Civil War. The best eatery in this area is **Vinegar Hill House** for its rustic American cuisine and lovely backyard garden [72 Hudson Ave].

The Mysterious House

239

Behind a gate at the end of Evans Street is a hidden white house that dates back to 1806. It originally belonged to the managers of the Brooklyn Navy Yard, New York's shipyard. The **Commander's Quarters** have been private property since 1964, and everyone wonders who the lucky owner is. There are often 1950s cars parked in the driveway, and the house was featured in the TV show *Boardwalk Empire* [24 Evans St].

You really don't want to eat your pizza with a knife and fork. New Yorkers eat the slices with their hands after folding them in half. #onlyinNY

Restaurants in the Bridges' Shadow

240

For a romantic evening, there's no place quite like **The River Café** with its enchanting decor. The restaurant opened its doors in 1977 in an old wharf, offering a perfect view of Manhattan and the Brooklyn Bridge. It feels like eating on the water, and the restaurant is surrounded by gardens where they often host weddings. The fixed-price menu costs $55 a person for brunch, $42 for lunch and $115 in the evening [1 Water St].

Gran Eléctrica serves authentic, high-end Mexican cuisine. The back terrace is in the shadow of the Manhattan Bridge. You can sip on habanero pepper-infused margaritas and taste some excellent ceviche. The wallpaper pays tribute to the 19th-century Mexican engraver and illustrator, José Guadalupe Posada [5 Front St].

At **Atrium**, Mediterranean-inspired market cuisine is featured in an industrial space. One of the restaurant's walls is covered in plants. The quinoa tagliatelle dish is one of my favorites [15 Main St].

The best pizza in DUMBO is at **Juliana's**. Don't be swayed by the line-up in front of Grimaldi's right next door, the pizza at Juliana's is much better [19 Old Fulton St].

Those with a sweet tooth can go to **One Girl Cookies**, the neighborhood go-to for cookies, cakes and cupcakes. The spacious spot is also a favorite with "laptop-ers" [33 Main St].

The House that Inspired the Author of *Breakfast at Tiffany's*

241 Famous American author **Truman Capote** lived in the yellow house at 70 Willow Street for a long time. Built in 1839, it's one of the oldest residences in the neighborhood. It has 18 rooms and a dozen fireplaces. In 2012, the house was sold for $12 million, a Brooklyn record at the time.

In 1955, Capote convinced the house's owner (theater producer Oliver Smith) to let him take a room. He stayed there for 10 years, drinking martinis on the veranda between writing sessions. That's where he wrote his greatest success, *Breakfast at Tiffany's*, as well as *A House on the Heights*. The latter is a story about his time in Brooklyn Heights: an area he felt was interwoven with "splendid contradictions."

The Promenade with a View of Manhattan

242 The esplanade that overlooks the Brooklyn-Queens Expressway is the crown jewel of Brooklyn Heights. At the end of the day, take advantage of the spectacular view of Manhattan, the Statue of Liberty and the Brooklyn Bridge. It's nicknamed **The Promenade**, and the entrance is at the corner of Orange Street and Columbia Heights. A tip for lovers of luxury houses: many stand tall at the end of the promenade on Remsen and Joralemon streets, as well as at Pierrepont Place.

The Italians of Brooklyn Heights

243 At Sardinian restaurant **River Deli** (A), where the exterior looks like an Edward Hopper painting, the charcuterie and cheese plates are served with Sardinia's classic, thin, crispy bread, the *pane carasau*. I recommend their pasta with lamb ragu [32 Joralemon St].

As for **Noodle Pudding** located near the Brooklyn Bridge, they serve excellent gnocchi, risotto, lasagna and osso buco. Ask for one of the tables by the window [38 Henry St].

244

A Trip Back in Time

244 It took five years before I visited the **New York Transit Museum**, and I regret not having gone sooner. The New York subway's museum is a must-see for those who wish to find out a bit more about the city's DNA. You'll learn about how, more than 100 years ago, they started to build what would become one of the largest subway systems in the world. Today there are 469 stations, 24 lines, 373 kilometers (232 miles) of rails and 5.5 million travelers a day.

Exhibited subway cars are from 1907, 1916, 1928 and 1949, just to name a few. You can come and go between them, and they still feature ads from their original eras. The museum is closed on Mondays and statutory holidays. It costs $7 to get in, and the entrance is at the intersection of Boreum Place and Schermerhorn Street in the old Clark Street station.

Brooklyn's Most Beautiful Neighborhood

245 **Brooklyn Heights** is a protected historical neighborhood with gorgeous houses, and one of the rare areas in Brooklyn that hasn't been overtaken by businesses. A few of its streets lined with some 2,000 trees are named after fruits like Cranberry, Orange and Pineapple. Grace Court Alley, Hunts Lane and Love Lane are old alleyways where they used to keep horses and carriages. Since then, stables have been turned into luxurious homes, making it a great spot for photos.

An oddity in the neighborhood is the Greek Revival-style house at **58 Joralemon Street** (A). Nobody lives there because the building has housed a subway airshaft since 1908, which is why the windows are boarded up with black panels.

245

245 A

Like in Thailand

246 Chef Andy Ricker is considered the *enfant terrible* of Thai cooking in New York, and the greatest ambassador of this cuisine that's unfortunately little known in the United States. Once a building laborer, Ricker fell in love with northern Thai cuisine during his many trips to Southeast Asia. He decided to open the restaurant **Pok Pok**, first in Portland (Oregon) and, since 2013, in Brooklyn near Cobble Hill's piers [117 Columbia St].

The Nostalgia Bar

247 **The Long Island Bar** was opened in an old diner that belonged to the same family since the 1950s. It closed in 2007 before being taken over by Toby Cecchini, a legend in the New York bartending scene. We can actually credit his inventiveness with the legendary cosmopolitan cocktail made famous in the TV show *Sex and the City*. Cecchini kept the restaurant's art deco style, as well as their neon sign. This place steeped in nostalgia mixes classic cocktails like the Boulevardier, and dishes out some food, including a delicious hamburger [110 Atlantic Ave]. In the same area, I also like **Grand Army**, an oyster bar that serves creative cocktails [336 State St].

The Pizza Haunt

248 Residents of Carroll Gardens will tell you that the best pizza can be had at **Lucali**, and I'm not about to disagree with them. This is a laid-back family spot located in an old candy store where you can bring your own wine. I love watching pizza chef Mark Iacono at work on a candlelit table at the back of the restaurant. He rolls out his dough using a wine bottle instead of a rolling pin. His pizzas and calzones are so delicious that you'll unfortunately have to wait in line. I recommend giving your name to the hostess and having a drink at **Bar Bruno** just two blocks away while you wait [520 Henry St]. The small Lucali pizzeria is open every day, except Tuesday, from 6 p.m. to 10 p.m. On weekends, they close at 11 p.m. [575 Henry St].

Smoked Meat Like in Montreal

249 **Mile End** is Noah Bernamoff's popular smoked meat restaurant. He's a Montrealer who has lived in New York for the last few years. He opened his delicatessen in an old garage in Boerum Hill in 2012, and it was an instant success. The decor in this narrow, 19-seat restaurant is entirely Montreal-inspired, with pictures of the city hanging on the walls [97A Hoyt St].

Fine Dining in Cobble Hill and Boerum Hill

250 Charming Spanish restaurant **La Vara** serves excellent tapas. The couple that owns it—Alexandra Raji and Eder Montero—are from the Basque Country. Order the fried artichokes, eggplant with honey and melted cheese, salted cod salad (with clementine, olives, pistachios, hard-boiled eggs and pomegranate seeds) and the olive oil ice cream [268 Clinton St].

Date nights are always a success at **Rucola**, a restaurant located on the ground floor of a brownstone house, where you can try northern Italian dishes. The lamb ragu on homemade pasta is divine [190 Dean St].

The Garden District

251 **Carroll Gardens** sets itself apart with its gardens in front of each house. When strolling along the two commercial thoroughfares—Court and Smith streets—you'll discover many old shopkeepers, butcher shops and Italian groceries, but also an increasing number of French businesses. This part of Brooklyn is actually nicknamed "Little France."

My favorite restaurant is **Frankies Spuntino** (A), an Italian bistro in an old social club where you can eat rustic, affordable cuisine. Regulars come in to read at the bar during the afternoon. The back terrace is one of the prettiest in town, so much so that couples get married there. They also have long tables to accommodate groups [457 Court St].

Proprietors Frank Castronovo and Frank Falcinelli also own the restaurant **Prime Meats** a few doors down, where inspiration comes from the Alps' Germanic cuisine. As its name suggests, this eatery that stocks up at local farms specializes in meat: beef tartar, pork chops, *rillettes*, pâté and homemade sausages [465 Court St].

252 A

253 A

Comfort Food in Carroll Gardens

252 Brunch at **Buttermilk Channel**—a restaurant that specializes in reinterpreted comfort food—is always popular. They make many types of Bloody Marys, scrambled eggs, buttermilk pancakes and a bacon-cheddar grilled cheese. For dinner, you can try duck meatloaf and fried chicken waffles. They also have a vegetarian menu, as well as one for kids. On Monday night, you'll order from a $30 menu, and Tuesday is BYOB [524 Court St].

When I'm in the mood for a good sandwich, I head to **Court Street Grocers** (A), a fine foods store with a takeout counter. Try the Delight (corned beef and Muenster), the Mother-in-Law (braised beef) or their grilled cheese [485 Court St]. I also love the sandwiches and pastries at **Smith Canteen**, a cafe established in a 100-year-old pharmacy [343 Smith St].

Another spot established in a 1920s pharmacy is **Brooklyn Farmacy & Soda Fountain**. They serve mostly desserts, including a dozen types of sundaes (The Elvis with banana, fudge and peanut butter is particularly delicious), old-school milk shakes and floats (a scoop of ice cream dunked in soda) [513 Henry St].

Eating Seafood in Red Hook

253 Red Hook was one of the liveliest ports in the world around 1920. Then, during the construction of the highways in the 1950s, the area was cut off from the rest of Brooklyn, and the port slowly lost its appeal. In the 1990s, the neighborhood (one of the most dangerous in the country at the time) was nicknamed the "crack capital of America." Since then, many artists have taken over the industrial warehouses, and New Yorkers now go there mostly to eat seafood. From Manhattan, the best way to get there is by taking the IKEA Water Taxi (see reason No. 9).

Red Hook Lobster Pound is worth the trip for their generous lobster sandwich alone. You can choose you crustacean straight from the tank [284 Van Brunt St].

The large **Fairway** (A) grocery sells lobster rolls that you can eat at the picnic tables in the back, from where you can see the Statue of Liberty [480-500 Van Brunt St].

On the other side of the street, the two-story seafood restaurant **Brooklyn Crab** is very popular due to its large terraces and mini golf. The decor is reminiscent of a Maine restaurant [24 Reed St].

Like in a Florida Motel

254 | Established in an old warehouse near the Gowanus Canal, **The Royal Palms** is the first New York shuffleboard club; a game usually associated with kitschy Fort Lauderdale motels. The 1,700-square-meter (18,300-square-foot) space with tropical decor has 10 courts that you can rent for $40 an hour (for four players). Beach chairs, tropical cocktail bars and food trucks complete the vibe. It's a unique spot to celebrate a birthday or have fun with a group on a rainy day. Evenings end with bingo parties hosted by drag queens [514 Union St].

255 256

The Workers' Sandwich Shop

255 Off the beaten path, **Defonte's** has been in business since 1922 for one simple reason: they make delicious, gargantuan sandwiches. Nick Defonte founded the family business. After arriving at Ellis Island, the Italian immigrant was unable to find work, so he decided to open a sandwich counter. In the early 1920s, the establishment fed many workers like longshoremen, firefighters, crane operators and truck drivers. Nowadays, his grandson Nicky is at the helm of this establishment patronized by many police officers from the local station. They serve 25 kinds of sandwiches on Italian rolls, some of them measuring nearly 25 centimeters (10 inches). The Dino, their meatball hero (another name for a submarine sandwich), is astounding [379 Columbia St].

Key West in Brooklyn

256 A visit to Red Hook would be incomplete without a stop at **Steve's Authentic Key Lime Pies**. For over 30 years, Steve Tarpin has made authentic key lime pies like those in Key West. He also sells individual mini pies on the spot. Try the Swingle, an iced lime tart on a stick, covered in melted chocolate. To find this spot, look for the PIES HERE sign [185 Van Dyke St]. Another unbelievable dessert place is the **Baked** bakery. Don't leave without trying their brownies or scones [359 Van Brunt St].

A Wine Warehouse in Red Hook

257 Yes, they've been making wine in Brooklyn since 2008. The owner of **Red Hook Winery**, Mark Snyder, convinced two winegrowers from Napa Valley to go on this adventure with him. They produce around 20 wines by stocking up on grapes from 15 New York wineries. You can taste the Red Hook Winery's products on-location for $5, every day from 11 a.m. to 5 p.m. (starting at noon on Sunday) [175-204, Van Dyke St, Pier 41, door 325 A].

The Sports and Entertainment Temple

258 Attending a Nets basketball game, Islanders hockey game or a concert at **Barclays Center** in Fort Greene is a unique experience. You'll never see spectators with as much style as at Barclays Center. I especially like the food court that features only Brooklyn restaurants, as well as the Fellow Barber barbershop. The general-purpose space with almost 18,000 seats was inaugurated in 2012. For the first time since the Dodgers baseball team left for Los Angeles in 1957, Brooklynites have professional teams, the NBA's Nets and the NHL's Islanders. All subway lines make it to the arena [620 Atlantic Ave].

Flea Market Shopping in Fort Greene

259 **Brooklyn Flea** is a flea market and food court of nearly 3,700 square meters (39,828 square feet) that takes place in a Fort Greene schoolyard every Saturday from 10 a.m. to 5 p.m., from April to November. It's the perfect spot to find antiques and vintage clothing, or to try a popsicle from **People's Pops**, an Asian-style hot dog at **Asiadog** or a grilled cheese from the popular **Milk Truck** (176 Lafayette Ave). If you're still hungry, stop in at **Graziella's**, an Italian restaurant nestled in an old garage. Their specialty is the arugula and Parmesan pizza [232 Vanderbilt Ave].

On your way out, don't miss the amazing campus at the **Pratt Institute** (the prestigious art and design college) at the intersection of Dekalb and Hall streets. The park is full of sculptures.

The Restaurant in a Pharmacy

260 **Locanda Vini e Olii** is one of the best restaurants in Clinton Hill. The Tuscan eatery is located in a 130-year-old pharmacy, the Lewis Drug Store. The owners kept the sign and wooden cabinets where they used to store medication. I like this place's laid-back atmosphere. If you're in the mood for a glass of wine, they'll simply leave the bottle at your table and measure what you drank at the end, using a stick [129 Gates Ave].

A Statue in the Parking Lot

261 Strangely enough, you can see a replica of the **Statue of Liberty** in the Brooklyn Museum's parking lot. It measures over 9 meters (30 feet)—the real statue is 46 meters (151 feet) high without the pedestal. William H. Flattau, a Russian auctioneer, commissioned this statue in 1902 for the roof of his building in the Upper West Side. It was his way of thanking the United States for welcoming him. It stayed there for 100 years before being relocated to the museum.

261

Brooklyn's Largest Museum

262 Upon exiting the subway in Eastern Parkway, I'm always impressed by this gigantic beaux-arts-style building from 1893, right in the heart of Prospect Heights. The **Brooklyn Museum** is often forgotten on the museum circuit, even though, with its 52,000 square meters (560,000 square feet) of exhibition space, it's the city's largest after the Metropolitan Museum of Art. The atmosphere is much more laid back here than at the Met. You can move chairs around and sit in front of the paintings you want to look at for a long time. The permanent collections include ancient Egyptian masterpieces, along with works of contemporary art. Don't miss their collection of 50 Rodin sculptures on the 5th floor.

The museum is closed on Monday and Tuesday. The institution closes at 11 p.m. on the first Saturday of the month (except in September). On those days, you can participate in all sorts of special activities, watch films, live music, exhibits, etc. It's a monthly party called the Target First Saturdays [200 Eastern Pkwy].

263

The Other Central Park

264 **Prospect Park** is a public park that measures over two square kilometers (585 acres). It was designed by landscape architects Calvert Vaux and Frederick Law Olmstead (the same person behind Central Park). Prospect Park is much wilder than Central Park; it's actually where you'll find the only forest in Brooklyn, The Ravine. You can also go horseback riding there, which is no longer possible in Central Park. Kensington Stables [51 Caton Pl] offers horseback riding lessons for kids and adults, from 7:30 a.m. to 8:30 p.m. every day, but you'll need to reserve a spot. As for horseback treks, they take place from 10 a.m. until sunset and cost $37 an hour per person (one person per horse).

Each Sunday, percussionists gather at Drummer's Grove. You can also rent paddleboats at the Lakeside LeFrak Center (and skate there in the winter) without having to wait in line like in Central Park. There's a carousel for kids that was made in 1912, as well as a zoo that's home to 400 animals of 80 different species. In the Children's Corner, there's an old farmhouse built by a Dutch family in the 18th century that's worth the trip. You have to use the Willink entrance at the intersection of Ocean and Flatbush avenues to access it.

The Superhero Store

264 Fifth Avenue in Park Slope between Flatbush Avenue and 15th Street is chock-full of independent and eclectic shops, but **Brooklyn Superhero Supply Co.** sets itself apart. Kids love this one-of-a-kind boutique that sells capes, costumes and superhero food (they even have an immortality potion!). Behind a secret door, you'll find a writing workshop for kids with learning disabilities that's hosted by volunteers [372 5th Ave].

The Eco-Friendly Pizza

265 I really like **Franny's** in Park Slope; it's an environmentally friendly pizzeria and Italian restaurant where all ingredients are from local producers. It's the kind of spot that would be at home in San Francisco. This establishment belongs to the couple that inspired the Slow Food movement in Berkeley, California: Andrew Feinberg and Francine Stephens. Most dishes are made up of only three or four ingredients. Try their olive oil and sea salt pizza; it's simple and delicious [348 Flatbush Ave]. The couple also owns **Rose's Bar & Grill** on the same avenue. There, you can taste the best cheeseburger and fries in Brooklyn [295 Flatbush Ave].

Brooklyn's Cherry Trees

266 Since the **Brooklyn Botanical Garden** is located right by the Brooklyn Museum, I usually visit both these places in the same day. Both the garden and museum are open year-round. The Japanese garden is beautiful in the winter, but not as much as during the cherry blossom season in April. For barely 10 days, the **Cherry Esplanade** that has about 200 cherry trees becomes a small heaven on Earth full of pink hues. The botanical garden is also home to a bonsai museum and perfume garden. The latter was inaugurated in 1955 and was the first garden in the country designed specifically for blind people. Some of its flowers— smell of chocolate or spearmint, for example—smell so strong that it's almost best to enjoy them with your eyes closed. There are two entrances: one at 990 Washington Avenue and the other at 150 Eastern Parkway.

The Restaurant Corridor

267 On Wythe Avenue, you'll find many good restaurants. For example, Mexican spot **Café de la Esquina** is located in an old, retro diner with a big terrace [225 Wythe Ave].

That said, one of my favorite spots remains **Cafe Mogador** (A): a Moroccan and Mediterranean restaurant that serves reasonably priced couscous and tagines. I especially like their brunch. Ask for a table in the atrium at the back [133 Wythe Ave]. Similarly, I also love **Zizi Limona** in Williamsburg [129 Havemeyer St].

For dessert and breakfast, I have a weak spot for **Bakeri** (B), a small Norwegian-inspired artisanal bakery with a lovely garden and fishpond [150 Wythe Ave].

267 A

267 B

The Hotel in an Old Cooperage

268

While nobody wanted to venture into this area in the past, Wythe Avenue—a main artery that runs along western Williamsburg—has been booming over the last few years. Restaurants, bars and hotels have already set up shop there. The arrival of the **Wythe Hotel** in 2012 definitely has something to do with it. After renovations that went on for five years, the boutique hotel in an old barrel manufacturer built in 1901 is now the heart of the neighborhood. The hotel has 72 rooms, some of which have bunk beds that were specially designed for touring bands who don't have the means to pay for individual rooms [80 Wythe Ave].

The **Reynard**, the hotel's restaurant, uses products from local farms, and many dishes are cooked over high heat in the huge open-concept kitchen. On the top floor, **The Ides** bar has a spectacular view of Manhattan, especially at the end of the day. Customers flock there to immortalize the sunset between the skyscrapers.

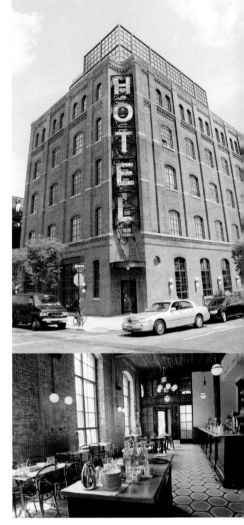

The worst time to look for a cab is between 4 p.m. and 5 p.m. during the work shift changeover, when the number of taxis drops by 20 percent on the streets of New York. Since 2013, new apple-green cabs ("boro taxis" or "boro cabs") service the neighborhoods where yellow taxis refuse to go. The green cabs can only pick up clients in the boroughs outside of Manhattan, such as Queens, the Bronx and Brooklyn, but also north of East 96th and West 110th streets in Manhattan. #onlyinNY

270A

A Night Out on Wythe Avenue

269 One of the neighborhood's only nightclubs, **Output**, attracts many renowned DJs. Spread out over two floors, the atmosphere is much more laid-back than in Manhattan's clubs in the Meatpacking District. However, you can't escape the $15 to $25 cover charges [74 Wythe Ave].

Next to the Wythe Hotel, you'll find **Kinfolk Studios**, an eclectic complex with multiple identities. It's a cafe, exhibition space and menswear shop during the day, turning into a bar, restaurant, concert venue and nightclub in the evening [90 and 94 Wythe Ave].

Not far from there, you can go bowling until 4 a.m. at **Brooklyn Bowl**. It's also a popular concert venue where they put on good shows with surprise guests. Their food is great; the fried chicken basket is legendary [61 Wythe Ave].

Brunch in Williamsburg

270 After a night of partying, brunch is a staple. One of the most popular destinations for it is **Five Leaves** (A) [18 Bedford Ave], just a stone's throw away from McCarren Park. Don't let the line discourage you, it moves quickly thanks to their numerous outdoor tables. There's a coffee counter outside to help keep you patient. Their most popular dishes are the crepes, Moroccan Scramble and ricotta appetizer to share (with figs, thyme, honey and salt) served with fruit bread and nuts.

Two other sure brunch bets are **Marlow & Sons** and **Diner**. They concoct rustic American cuisine that puts farm-fresh products in the spotlight. The two restaurants are side-by-side and belong to Williamsburg celebrity chef Andrew Tarlow. Diner is nestled in an old restaurant-wagon [81 Broadway], while Marlow & Sons is also a bar and general store [85 Broadway].

Everything is homemade at **Egg** where they serve breakfasts inspired by the American south to fried-food nuts. The restaurant is known for their Biscuits & Gravy, and there's a glass full of crayons on every table. Even adults can't resist the urge to draw on the white paper tablecloths [109 N 3rd St].

When it comes to comfort food, there's nowhere like **Pies 'n' Thighs** in this neighborhood. Pies—especially the apple one—doughnuts and fried chicken waffles are the specialties at this pretension-free restaurant located right at the exit of the Williamsburg Bridge [166 S 4th St].

The Princes of Chocolate

271 A tip for chocolate lovers: **Mast Brothers** is worth the trip, if only to breathe in the smell that fills the artisanal chocolate shop. Brothers Rick and Michael Mast—two bearded guys from Iowa—make refined chocolate bars with a dozen different flavors. My favorite is the Sea Salt bar. Their patterned wrappers are as pretty as the chocolate inside is good [111A N 3rd St].

The Mast brothers also own a unique spot a few doors down, **The Brew Bar**, a chocolate brewing bar. You can choose from many types of cocoa beans that are then ground up and brewed like coffee. The result is surprising, not at all bitter, but quite different from the hot chocolate of your childhood. The Dominican Republic brew has a slight tobacco flavor, while the Peru one has notes of cinnamon, molasses and fruit, and Papua New Guinea's is both fruity and smoky. It's a whole new way to enjoy chocolate [105A N 3rd St].

272 274

The Artists' Bookstore

272 If you have an artistic soul, you need to check out the **Brooklyn Art Library**, headquarters of the Sketchbook Project, a digital library that contains the notebooks of nearly 16,000 artists from over 130 countries. You can consult them free of charge and dive into the creative world of a professional artist, grandmother or six-year-old child. They also sell many beautiful albums of New York, paper and office supplies. The library also serves as a relaxing reading room [103A N 3rd St].

The Record Store that Refuses to Die

273 **Rough Trade** is an anachronism. The huge 1,400-square-meter (15,070-square-foot) store opened its doors in November 2013 in one of New York's most expensive neighborhoods. Since all the other record stores were shutting down, it was quite a gamble. This is the first American branch of the popular London store that was established 1976. The Brooklyn space is a CD and vinyl shop, but also a music venue, cafe run by the popular restaurant Five Leaves, and a bar [64 N 9th St].

Foodie Paradise

274 Every Saturday afternoon from spring to fall, the outdoor **Smorgasburg** market attracts big crowds. The fair presents 100 or so artisan kiosks and a bunch of local restaurants. It's the birthplace of many culinary trends, such as the ramen burger. You'll also find a few antique sellers and vintage shops. The market is by the water where you can catch an amazing glimpse of Manhattan [90 Kent Ave].

The Best Coffee in Williamsburg

275 **Toby's Estate** is a roaster, cafe, shop space, and espresso-tasting laboratory open to the public, all rolled into one. You can also take coffee classes here. I love this place first and foremost for its airy decor and shelves filled with knickknacks [125 N 6th St].

For a more authentic experience, **Caffe Capri** (A) serves the best ice coffee in town. The charming Italian owners, Sarah Devita and Joe Rinaldi, make it with crushed ice. They've been in business since 1974 and are beloved neighborhood characters. They also sell delicious homemade cannoli [427 Graham Ave].

The Steak You Won't Forget

276 Founded in 1887, **Peter Luger** is an option for special occasions, since their steak for two costs $99.95. Get the porterhouse with a side of spinach. You really shouldn't order your steak well-done; you'll be treated to comments from the waiter [178 Broadway].

Argentinian restaurant El Almacen and the St. Anselm also serve excellent steaks that are more affordable and still very high quality. These two neighborhood eateries have rustic decor with soft lighting and a predominance of wood.

At **El Almacen**, the Costilla de Res—a malbec-braised beef rib—has made a name for itself. To enjoy it in a pretty setting, ask for a table in the garden [557 Driggs Avenue].

At **St. Anselm**, the Butchers Steak with a side of iceberg salad topped with bacon vinaigrette wins the grand prize. The pea and grilled halloumi salad or the grilled avocados stuffed with aioli shrimp are also delicious [355 Metropolitan Ave].

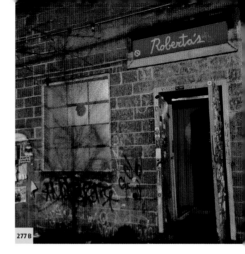

277 B

The Best Pizza in Williamsburg

277 For a simple slice to go, you have to stop in at **Best Pizza** (A). The walls at this charming pizzeria are covered with paper plates decorated by customers [33 Havemeyer St]. For a more complete experience, **Motorino** [139 Broadway] and **Roberta's** (B) [261 Moore St] are two top destinations. Roberta's is located in an industrial section of East Williamsburg. In the summer, you can eat in the vegetable garden out back. With all the furniture made out of recycled materials, it feels like being in a commune.

275 A 277 A

Williamsburg's Bars

278

Williamsburg, along with Manhattan's East Village, is probably the New York neighborhood with the most bars. I often go to **Hotel Delmano** (A), a cocktail bar where the walls are covered with old portraits and antique mirrors. The best seats in the house are at the leather booth or on the pretty terrace. Their Brooklyn Beauty cocktail is exquisite [82 Berry St].

Those who prefer their drinks in mugs can go to Austrian-inspired bar **Radegast Hall & Biergarten**. They sell two-dozen types of beer on tap and over 80 in bottles. They serve Eastern European dishes and barbecued sausages [113 N 3rd St]. At **Spuyten Duyvil**, Belgian beer is the specialty. This place is very popular thanks to its garden that's one of the most beautiful in Brooklyn [359 Metropolitan Ave].

The Gutter (B) is a dark, retro bowling alley from the 1970s. Everything is vintage here: the eight lanes, photos on the walls, lamps, leather armchairs, arcade games and even the Coca-Cola sign outside. The bar has 12 kinds of draft beer. A game will set you back $7, with an extra $3 for shoe rental [200 N 14th St].

Miss Favela is a Brazilian resto-bar with an atmosphere like no other, especially during summer nights when customers dance between the tables. It feels like being on vacation [57 S 5th St].

Located in an old swimming pool accessories store, the **Union Pool** bar has a decor reminiscent of the 1960s. It's very popular in the summertime due to its large patio where you'll find a parked taco truck [484 Union Ave].

To discover new wines, I like **The Four Horsemen**, the natural wine bar owned by James Murphy, former member of the band LCD Soundsystem [295 Grand St].

A tip for arcade game lovers: **Barcade** has about 50 vintage video game consoles, including the famous Tetris. Each game costs 25 cents, like in the good old days. The bar that was established in 2004 in an old metalworking shop only serves local beers on tap [388 Union Ave].

278A 278B

280 A   280 B

A Romantic Night in Williamsburg

279 Restaurant **Maison Première** is inspired by New Orleans' speakeasies and has one of the most romantic terraces in town. Oysters are served on old-fashioned silver platters and cocktails come in vintage glasses [298 Bedford Ave].

For sushi lovers, **1 OR 8**—a restaurant with all-white decor—is the perfect spot for a romantic date [66 S 2nd St].

The Japanese tavern **Cherry Izakaya** concocts many succulent sharing-sized dishes. For more privacy, request a small, private room in the mezzanine. The decor is inspired by 1970s Tokyo, with wooden panels, hand-painted murals and vintage pachinko (a type of Japanese pinball) at the entrance [138 N 8th St].

The New Graffiti Mecca

280 As Williamsburg rents skyrocket, artists increasingly move east toward Bushwick. The neighborhood that once had a bad reputation is now undergoing a full transformation. **The Bushwick Collective** (A) group—founded in 2012 by a neighborhood resident—got the idea to ask business owners to reserve one of their exterior walls for international artists. This is how Troutman Street became the biggest mural gallery in New York. Graffiti artists practice their craft here in a completely legal fashion and, as a result, you can see about 50 works of art that change with the seasons [L subway line, Jefferson Street station].

Plan a stop at **AP Café** (B) in this neighborhood so that you can enjoy a coffee, smoothie, sandwich, salad or tacos. With its modern, airy design, AP reminds me of the cafes of Silver Lake in Los Angeles [420 Troutman St].

A Neighborhood that Marches to the Beat of Its Own Drum

281 I love **Greenpoint** at the northern tip of Brooklyn for its industrial, waterfront look, but especially because you can stroll down tree-lined streets without seeing anyone. It's one of last remaining New York neighborhoods that isn't packed, since it's only served by one subway line (the infamous G line, loathed by New Yorkers due to its irregular service). The area's most interesting drag is Franklin Street. Have breakfast at **Le Gamin**, a charming French restaurant that specializes in sweet and savory crepes, omelets and baguette sandwiches [108 Franklin St]. **Transmitter Park**, located along the East River in an old industrial zone at the end of Greenpoint Avenue, has a breathtaking view of Manhattan.

The Restaurant in an Old Glass Factory

282 In my opinion, **Glasserie** is Greenpoint's most beautiful restaurant and the one that's most worth the trip to this off-the-beaten-track area. It was established in an old glass factory built in 1860 by the water, at Brooklyn's northern border next to Long Island City. Young chef Sara Kramer cooks up rustic Middle Eastern dishes with modern touches. Give in to their lamb cakes and homemade Yemeni bread. I recommend this spot for both brunch and dinner [95 Commercial St].

Grabbing a Drink in Greenpoint

283 **Ramona**, a cocktail bar with a room on the upper floor [113 Franklin St], and **Alameda,** where cocktails are served in old glasses at a gorgeous horseshoe-shaped bar [195 Franklin St], are my two favorite hangouts. **Achilles Heel**, one of restaurateur Andrew Tarlow's many establishments, offers a hybrid concept: they serve pastries and coffee in the morning, followed by cocktails, *charcuterie* plates, oysters and sandwiches at night. They've kept the early 1900s tavern decor intact [180 West St]. **Northern Territory**—an Australian resto-bar with a rooftop terrace—is very popular at the end of the day due to the stunning view of Manhattan that's its greatest attraction [12 Franklin St].

Paulie's Pizza

284 Paul Gianonne, an old manager at AT&T, decided to leave his job one day and devote himself to his true passion. He built a wood-burning oven in his New Jersey backyard and started cooking pizzas for the neighborhood. Word of mouth did its part, and he finally opened his own restaurant in Greenpoint, **Paulie Gee's**, in 2010. Their menu lists about 30 different pizzas, including eight vegetarian ones. Try the Greenpointer with fresh mozzarella, arugula, olive oil, lemon and Parmesan shavings (Parma ham can be added for $3). If you're not in the mood to wait for a table to free up, order a pie to go and have a picnic in Transmitter Park at the end of the street [60 Greenpoint Ave].

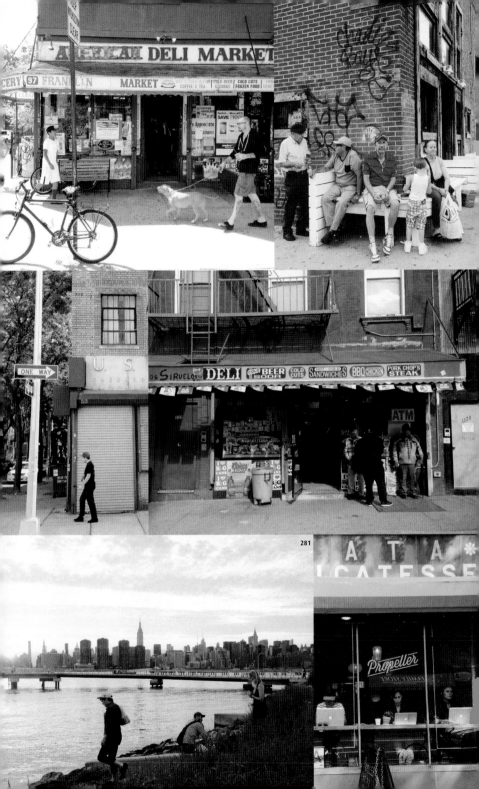

281

The Apartment-Hotel

285

For those looking to get away from Manhattan for a bit, the **Box House Hotel** offers mini apartments as rooms. Some even have a terrace with a view of Manhattan, while others are equipped with a mezzanine. An old taxi from the 1970s parked in front of the door can drive you around the surrounding area for free. The hotel also provides a shuttle to the ferry that can get you to Manhattan in just a few minutes by crossing the East River. Room prices start at $189 a night for a stay of at least three nights [77 Box St].

The Hip Bed-and-Breakfast

286

Urban Cowboy—an old townhouse converted into a bed-and-breakfast with a modern design—has a unique experience in store for its guests (urbancowboybnb.com). Along with the four upstairs bedrooms and a large communal room with an open-concept kitchen, they also have a cabin in the yard (Kanoono Cabin) with decor worthy of a cottage in the Adirondacks. It comes equipped with a king-sized bed, kitchenette and bathtub (approximately $400 a night). Single rooms cost about $100 a night, while doubles go for $200 [111 Powers St].

287 288

The Time Machine

287

To discover another side of New York, **The City Reliquary** showcases a collection of 100 or so objects connected to New York's history, such as terra-cotta fragments of emblematic buildings, subway tokens, baseball cards, pizza boxes from all eras and relics of New York's 1939 World Fair. Most artifacts are donated by New Yorkers [370 Metropolitan Ave].

If Brooklyn were a city, it would be the fourth largest in the United States due to its population. One-third of New Yorkers live in the borough, meaning 2.6 million residents. The name "Brooklyn" comes from Breucklelen (now Breukelen), an old Dutch town. #onlyinNY

The Boardwalk's Dancers

288

Coney Island's beach is relatively clean, and its **boardwalk** is far more authentic than Atlantic City's. I recommend going in the spring or early summer because this place gets very busy by late June, after the Mermaid Parade. Get there directly by subway, taking the D, F, N and Q trains.

You'll rub shoulders with locals, colorful characters, old Eastern European couples and the famous boardwalk dancers. The latter founded an association in 1996 and get together every weekend where they dance on the dock to house and soul DJ music.

You might see **Tony Disco**, a wonderful mix of Elvis and Tony Manero (John Travolta's character in *Saturday Night Fever*). Tony Disco is over 80 years old and dances wearing a white fedora and Hawaiian shirt.

The Vacation District

289

There's something magical about taking the subway in Manhattan and ending up in a completely different universe 45 minutes later, far from the city's chaos. For the mere price of a subway ticket, you can treat yourself to a vacation day at **Coney Island**, a one-time island that became a peninsula at the southern tip of Brooklyn.

The **Luna Park** amusement park faces the Atlantic Ocean. Unlike at chain parks like Six Flags that are fenced-in enclaves closed off from the world, Coney Island's is open and free of charge. The wooden Cyclone is Luna Park's most famous ride, and it's still terrifying despite being 88 years old. The first drop is 26 meters (85 feet) high, and the train turns corners at 60 kilometers (37 miles) an hour. In the summer of 2014, they inaugurated a new roller coaster, the Thunderbolt, with a train that goes up to 88 kilometers (55 miles) an hour.

The Legendary Hot Dog

290

A visit to Coney Island wouldn't be complete without stopping in at the famous **Nathan's** hot dog stand that was founded in 1916 by Polish immigrant Nathan Handwerker. The establishment is a part of New York's multicultural heritage. A huge sign on the side of the building displays the number of days before the next annual hot dog eating contest. Hundreds of people participate in it on Independence Day, every 4th of July. In 2014, the winner Joey Chestnut devoured 61 hot dogs in 10 minutes. Guaranteed to make you stomach turn! [1310 Surf Ave].

Coney Island's Best Pizza

291

The Neapolitan pizzeria **Totonno's**—where the walls are decorated with photos of Joe DiMaggio, Lou Reed and other notorious characters—has belonged to the same family since 1924. Antonio "Totonno" Pero's business has survived many disasters since it opened, including a big fire in 2009, as well as the ravages of Hurricane Sandy in 2012. Their pizza is some of the best in town (the mozzarella is homemade and the tomatoes are from Italy). Totonno's is open from Thursday to Sunday inclusively, from noon to 8 p.m., but they close up shop once they run out of pizza dough [1524 Neptune Ave].

The Russian Neighborhood

292

From Coney Island, you can get to **Brighton Beach** by walking about 10 minutes down the boardwalk, which is one of my favorite strolls. Along the beach, the red brick buildings are home to the largest Russian diaspora outside of Moscow. It's a total culture shock. I like to sit on large terraces facing the sea, including the one at kitschy restaurant **Tatiana** (A) [3152 Brighton 6th St, the entrance is on the boardwalk]. You can head back to Manhattan by taking the subway in Brighton Beach [B or Q lines].

289 292A

292

290

The Godfather of Pizza

293

In the Midwood neighborhood where Woody Allen grew up, you will find the Di Fara Pizza, owned by Dom DeMarco. The pizza chef, now in his seventies, is known as "the godfather of New York pizza." Some say that he makes the best pizza in the entire East Side. For the past 50 years, he has set to work with the same enduring passion.

"Buon giorno, veni, veni!" he greets me, his blue eyes sparkling and his hands covered in white flour. I slip behind the counter, next to an old rusty cash register, to get a better view of his work. The room can get as hot as 50°C (122°F), and there is olive oil everywhere. The space hasn't changed since 1964; the walls are lined with glowing newspaper reviews and old, yellowed photographs of Italy.

Nestled at the corner of Avenue J and East 15th Street, in a rather unremarkable neighborhood, Di Fara's huge success remains a mystery, even to Dom DeMarco: "Who would have thought that a pizza counter would survive in a Jewish neighborhood?" Manhattan is 45 minutes away by subway, yet people come from as far as Japan, London and Florida to line up outside the place—and despite the two-hour wait, nobody complains. DeMarco insists on making each pizza himself, and he writes down the orders on paper plates. No one but him touches the ingredients or the oven, and he can make up to 150 pizzas a day. He uses old-fashioned tools and takes the pizzas out of the oven with his bare hands. It's hard to find a more authentic pizza experience than this, and he tends to view all other restaurants as imposters.

Di Fara is also the most expensive pizza in New York. One slice costs $5 and a whole pizza costs at least $28. "All my ingredients are imported from Italy, and the cost of transportation is rising, so I have no choice," he explains matter-of-factly.

And this is precisely Dom DeMarco's secret: he only uses ingredients that come from Caserta, his hometown near Naples. Twice a week, he receives a shipment of flour, olive oil, fresh San Marzano tomatoes, and mozzarella di bufala. "Very fresh," he says, while spreading a generous amount of mozzarella over the dough. The basil, which he cuts by hand with old scissors, comes from Israel. He finishes it all off with a lot of olive oil and a big handful of grana padano (a traditional cow's milk cheese). Pizza is his entire life. "I will keep going until I can't walk anymore." The restaurant is open from Wednesday to Sunday (1424 Ave J).

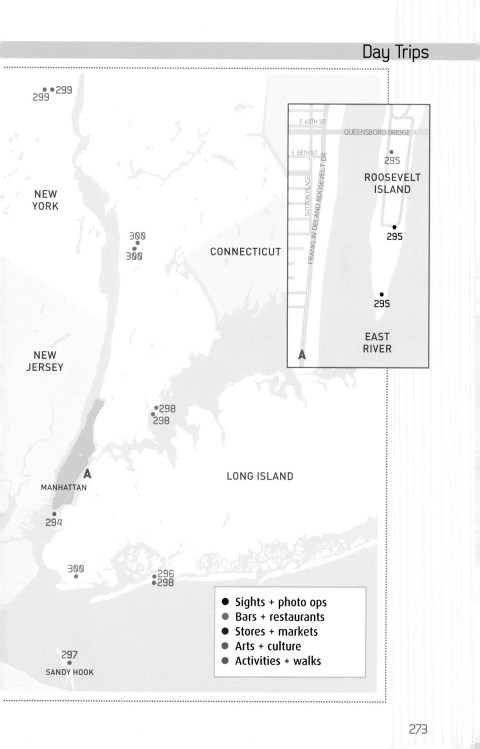

299 •299

E 60TH ST

QUEENSBORO BRIDGE

E 58TH ST

295

ROOSEVELT
ISLAND

NEW
YORK

SUTTON PLACE

FRANKLIN DELANO ROOSEVELT DR

295

300

300

CONNECTICUT

295

EAST
RIVER

NEW
JERSEY

A

298
298

A

MANHATTAN

LONG ISLAND

294

300

296
298

● Sights + photo ops
● Bars + restaurants
● Stores + markets
● Arts + culture
● Activities + walks

297

SANDY HOOK

294

295A

ROOSEVELT ISLAND

295B

Getaway Island

294

Governors Island is one of my favorite getaways. Located south of Manhattan, the small island is only open to the public during the summer season (late May to late September). It's accessible by ferry; the ride leaving from the Battery Maritime Building lasts just a few minutes [10 South St]. A round-trip ticket costs $2 (free for children).

Governors Island, nicknamed "Alcatraz of the East," was used as a military base up until the 1960s. Castle Williams was built in 1807 on the northwest side of the island in case of a British invasion.

This place was closed off to the public until the City of New York transformed the island into a public space in 2005. The $250 million project breathed new life into the abandoned military buildings. Now, the space has many playgrounds, art installations, two baseball fields, a hedge maze, a thicket with 50 hammocks and walking paths.

It's a great place to look out at the Statue of Liberty without the tourist crowds, to bike (you can rent one on the spot or bring your own on the ferry), watch an outdoor concert or have a picnic.

The best time to go is during the Jazz Age Lawn Party when they celebrate the roaring twenties. Participants dress up and dance to the music of the Dreamland Orchestra in an atmosphere worthy of *The Great Gatsby*. There's also a pie contest, a 1920s car exhibit and dance classes. The event takes place over two weekends, in June and August (jazzagelawnparty.com).

Ruins and a Memorial

295

A narrow island in the East River located between Manhattan and Queens, **Roosevelt Island** was known, until the mid 20th century, as a very impoverished island (people called it Welfare Island). They only had hospitals, prisons and asylums. Since the 1970s, the island has seen a residential development that now houses approximately 14,000 residents. This number could see some growth over the next 20 years, as Cornell University plans on making the island home to its all-new technology institute campus.

The island also boasts New York's most famous ruins. **The Smallpox Hospital** (A), founded in 1856, is a neo-Gothic establishment that was abandoned in the 1950s. They're the city's only ruins registered with the National Register of Historic Places. If you've seen the romantic comedy *For Love or Money* (1993) starring Michael J. Fox, it's the building that Doug Ireland wants to convert into a hotel.

At the southern tip of the island, you'll find the **Franklin D. Roosevelt Four Freedoms Park** memorial (B), which was about 40 years in the making. Unveiled in 2012, it was designed by the famous American architect Louis Kahn who died in 1974.

The best (and most fun) way to get to Roosevelt Island is to take the red cable car at the corner of East 60th Street and 2nd Avenue in Manhattan from Tramway Plaza to the Roosevelt Island Tram Station. You can also get there by subway [F train, Roosevelt Island station].

Hipsters and Surfers

296

Queens' **Rockaway Beach** inspired the famous Ramones song. It's also the largest public beach in the United States, and the only one in New York where you can surf legally. It therefore welcomes a large surfer community, as well as many restaurant stands along the boardwalk, including the one located around 105th Street. It's sort of like the on-the-sea version of Williamsburg in Brooklyn.

Unfortunately, the community was largely destroyed by Hurricane Sandy in October 2012, but is slowly rebuilding itself. The beaches were restored, and new restaurants and hotels have opened their doors. That's the case for **Playland**, a 12-room motel erected on the ruins of a 19th-century building ravaged by the storm. A Brooklyn artist decorated each room—one of which has a bed under a tipi. The terrace covered in sand and colorful beach chairs is very popular during the summertime for its guest DJs. It's the kind of place you go to party rather than rest. Room prices vary between $60 on weeknights and $250 during weekends [97-20 Rockaway Beach Blvd].

Popular restaurant **Tacoway Beach** is a surfer favorite. This place is both hip and bohemian, and gives some soul to the dilapidated neighborhood. They serve excellent fish, chorizo or tofu tacos for $3.50 a piece. The stand is located inside the **Rockaway Beach Surf Club** [3-02 Beach 87th St].

You can get to Rockaway Beach by subway (on the A train) or on the ferry that leaves from Pier 11 at Wall Street on weekends and holidays. A round-trip costs $30; one-way is $20 [newyorkbeachferry.com].

The White Sand Beach with a View of Manhattan

297

Sandy Hook is technically in New Jersey, but it's a very popular spot with New Yorkers looking to escape the crushing August humidity. Sandy Hook is a 12-kilometer (7½-mile) peninsula where European colonists landed in 1609. The lighthouse dates back to 1764.

The many public, white-sand beaches are accessible by ferry from southern Manhattan; the ride takes 40 minutes with the company Seastreak (seastreak.com/ sandyhook.aspx). The beaches are monitored and have snack bars, bathrooms and showers. Know that one of the beaches, **Gunnison Beach**, is a nudist beach. The best way to explore Sandy Hook is by bike. You can bring your own on the ferry or rent one there.

298

Seafood Island

298

City Island is nicknamed "The Hamptons of the Bronx." The little-known island is mostly visited during the summer for its many competing seafood restaurants on the main thoroughfare, City Island Avenue. Just over 4,000 people live on the small island that measures 2.5 kilometers (1½ miles) by one kilometer (½ mile). Most of them are families that stay there from generation to generation. It's a fisherman island where you can see a few 100-year-old houses, many of which could unfortunately use some upkeep. Several movies were filmed on City Island, including *Awakenings* starring Robert De Niro and Robin Williams, and Wes Anderson's *The Royal Tenenbaums*.

Johnny's Reef is at the southern tip of the island. The cafeteria-style restaurant hasn't changed since the 1950s. Feast on fish and chips, shrimp and fried calamari, and grilled lobster at one of the many picnic tables facing Eastchester Bay [2 City Island Ave]. You can get there by public transit by taking the 6 train and getting off at the last station [Pelham Bay Park], with an approximately 10-minute connecting ride on the BX29 bus.

300

Recharging Your Batteries on a Farm

300 I usually combine a stroll through the **Storm King Art Center** with a visit to the **Stone Barns Center for Food & Agriculture**. This gourmet destination is very popular with New Yorkers and is a focal point for New York's Slow Food movement. The 80-hectare piece of land—located about 45 minutes north of Manhattan in Westchester County—has a farm, a restaurant in an amazing stone barn from the 1930s and an educational center. The Rockefeller family financed the $30 million project.

This place is open year-round, from Wednesday to Sunday. Families love the chicken coop, sheep pen and greenhouses. A cafe with a large terrace allows you to savor daily specials made with products from the farm. They also have a dinnerware shop.

To dine at **Blue Hill**—a reputed restaurant by chef Dan Barber who was also one of the instigators of the Farm-to-Table movement in the United States—it's best to make a reservation two months ahead of time. The tasting menu costs between $138 and $198. However, it's also possible to eat at the bar, where the menu is a bit less pricey, without a reservation. You can also visit the sumptuous Rockefeller family mansion, **Kykuit**, located nearby. Reserve your tickets at: hudsonvalley.org [200 Lake Road].

The Sculpture Park

299 When you're on the road just north of New York, make a stop at the **Storm King Art Center**. It's a huge 200-hectare sculpture park located about 75 minutes north of Manhattan in the Hudson Valley. The open-air contemporary art museum boasts about 100 giant sculptures by artists like Louise Bourgeois, Alexander Calder, Roy Lichtenstein, David Smith, Richard Serra and Isamu Noguchi.

The scenery alone—peppered with sculpted hills, plains and forests—is worth the trip. The best way to explore the grounds remains by bike; you can rent one there. Plan about two hours for the visit. Admission costs $15 for adults and $8 for kids between the ages of 5 and 18 [1 Museum Rd, New Windsor]. Coach USA can also get you there from Manhattan's Port Authority Bus Terminal.

index

Index numbers do not refer to page numbers, but to the 300 Reasons to Love New York.

acknowledgments

Many thanks are owed to the whole team at Éditions de l'Homme who allowed me to make this great dream come true. A special thank you to my editor, Élizabeth Paré, for her endless patience, sound advice, and for helping me to get my New York mess organized. Thanks to Sylvain Trudel for his vigilance, passion for the project and eagle eye. Thanks to Diane Denoncourt and Josée Amyotte who brought this book to life with so much style. Finally, thank you to Quebecor management for trusting me during my years as a New York correspondent.

This guidebook would not have been possible without the support of my family and my New York accomplice, Geoffrey, with whom I discovered the city, one adventure at a time.